Contents

Introduction

This book is intended for two main groups of readers: aspiring senior managers in schools, currently in middle management positions; and existing deputy and assistant headteachers, who want to reflect on their own practice. The book could also be useful to ambitious teachers near the beginning of their careers, interested in seeing what the key issues of senior management in their schools are.

The varying contexts of senior management teams

This book sets out to examine what it takes to do a good job as a school senior manager. It focuses on being a member of a senior management team and not the leader of it, that is to say headteacher. Obviously, many members of senior management teams (SMTs) will go on to become headteachers themselves, but while they are serving in a team of assistant and deputy headteachers in a large secondary school or as the sole deputy in a primary school, they have to take on the responsibilities delegated to them by their boss – the headteacher. The job combines 'leading' and 'supporting'. This blend of subordination and initiative-taking can be an awkward and challenging role to do well.

In our current climate of managerialism, there is a quest to meet a constant stream of school improvement targets. The tendency to deny the reality of the true level of difficulties that sections of the pupil intake have to contend with on the basis that 'nothing is impossible' if a school is well managed and led puts tremendous pressure on headteachers to achieve the unthinkable. They can offload this anxiety onto their nearest colleagues – their senior managers. So the vital 'x' factor for being a senior manager anywhere is not to offload yourself further down the chain of command but to try and stay relaxed, remembering to be empathetic with the people you work with. The more emotional and intellectual honesty you bring to the job, the more valuable your contribution will end up being.

Often forgotten in a era of long institutional development plans is that senior managers need to get the best out of teachers and pupils in classrooms. To have a chance of success at this, you need to have the spirit of innovation in you and the tendency to be imaginative and proactive. There is no point obtaining a senior position in a school if you intend to use your new level of power and influence to 'tread water' and apply the same old tired solutions to problems that have prevailed for years.

If you have been a good middle manager as a head of year or as a head of department, you will have already been a positive and improving force in your area of responsibility. This will have entailed holding onto good existing practice in your team of teachers and seeking intelligent ways to improve what that group of professionals does and how they do it. Broadly speaking, senior management needs these same skills, only with broader brush strokes over a larger remit of school life. So, where you've been accustomed to lead on assessment and reporting in your own area, you might find yourself thinking and planning for a system that will be used school-wide. This concept will be referred to in this book as whole-school management.

Different types of school

There is no blueprint for describing what the senior management experience is going to be like. The flavour of it will be very different in the many varieties of school up and down the country. Being a senior team member at a girls' grammar school in Kent may have a very different set of challenges to becoming a deputy headteacher in an inner-city boys' school in London, where half the pupils have free school meals and 100 different languages are spoken. Some schools have a fight or serious disorder twice a day and others once a year or almost never. In some schools senior managers are asked to deal with high levels of verbal and physical abuse on a daily basis. In others, the most serious crime is a non-school-uniform nose ring, the wrong coloured shoes or a failure to finish homework.

Each and every school has an intake that is truly individual and each one offers a very different experience of leadership and management. If you are an aspiring senior manager you may feel versatile enough to deal with any challenge that is put in your path, but others may feel apprehensive about going to a very academic or a very behaviourally challenging school. Making a decision about how flexible you can be is vital in your job applications.

Different types of headteacher

Wherever you become a senior manager, the personality of your headteacher can make or break your working life. A good head-teacher will play to your strengths and give you lots of chances to work autonomously and creatively. A poor headteacher could bear down on you with petty dictatorial demands and delegate an excessive workload to you. In a negative situation with a persis-tently poor relationship with a headteacher, it doesn't matter what brilliance you have as an aspiring senior manager. No matter how difficult, it is vital to keep working to achieve a reasonable relationship with the 'boss' and hold onto it, whatever the cost to your desire for reform, innovation and creativity. Without the headteacher's overall support and backing, you cannot do any part of your job well. We will return to the business of building and maintaining relationships with the headteacher in Chapter 5.

What is clear is that being a member of senior management and not the headteacher of a school calls for particular qualities of leadership and management. General principles and good practice still apply, but being a subordinate leader is not the same as being the truly anointed commander in chief.

Different personalities within the senior management team

The majority of teachers come to senior management posts from middle management of a large department or year group in a secondary school. In primary schools, they may have been a subject leader or held responsibility for a key whole-school area of teaching such as literacy. A few professionals come from advisory teacher roles or inspector jobs with local authorities. Fewer still may come from the world of teacher-training colleges, having been teachers before they became lecturers.

Senior management teams need people with certain common key skills of leadership and management, as we shall see in this book. But there are many different ways of operating within these core competencies. So you can be laid back, bossy, reserved, pedantic about detail, beautifully empathetic, predominantly intuitive or largely analytical and there will be a place for you in a school somewhere. Given that senior managers work in teams, there is always a need for a variety of personalities in a team, bringing with them a large range of personal strengths and hopefully a way of making up for each other's shortcomings.

My personal experience as basis for self-reflection and case study

In this book I shall draw upon my own experience of middle management in four London schools and then senior management in three others, over the last twenty years. Each chapter will include examples of real-life situations that represent the kind of scenarios you might be asked to deal with on a regular basis. We will explore the issue for senior school leaders that arise from them, sometimes looking at the mistakes I made and how I learned lessons from them. All names and places will be disguised so as not to cause unintended offence to the people I have worked alongside.

Divergence between primary and secondary school senior management

Obviously there is no hiding the fact that all my experience is in secondary school, so I have talked to a number of primary senior managers to try and pick out explicit points of difference in their daily leadership and management experiences. Where appropriate, I will have a section in each chapter that deals with these specific differences of role and expectation. Not surprisingly, the vast majority of the leadership and management issues are the same.

School policy

You will come across many difficult situations as a senior manager, and a key issue will be dealing with disruptive pupils. There are rules and laws about dealing with pupils and you must make sure you know the content and meaning of the latest versions, coupled with a detailed knowledge and understanding of your own school policy.

How to use this book

This book is essentially set out in two sections, the first two chapters consider the 'Getting in' part of the title – the ways in which you can plan ahead to become a senior manager. They describe how to prepare yourself as a middle manager to be successful in the application and selection processes.

The rest of the book is about 'Getting on' once you've got the promotion. This includes detailed practical information on how to embark on your new career, without falling flat on your face in front of the pupils and staff in the first term.

Subsequently, each chapter focuses on the accumulation of skills you need to become a good senior manager. These chapters describe the expertise needed to handle the difficult scenarios that the stakeholders in the school community present each day. This can vary from difficult parents to wily inspectors, and from confrontational dinner supervisors to drunken pupils.

If you choose to read the text from cover to cover, you can follow the whole process from ambitious middle manager to assured senior colleague. But it should be easy to pick the book up and read a part of a chapter as reference material on a particular problem.

No senior manager can be successful unless they accumulate a strong working knowledge of all their school's policies on the important aspects of daily life, especially the ones that relate to health and safety and child protection in the workplace. So each time a new senior leader finds themselves in a new situation, reading documents on procedures as well as consulting colleagues and the headteacher are vital.

Part I

Getting into senior management

Chapter 1

Preparing for a senior management position

In this chapter we look at:

- the knowledge you need to prepare yourself for school senior management;
- the absolutely essential and highly desirable career experiences you need to prepare yourself for a promotion.

No two people's career development and aspirations are the same. Person specifications for senior management usually demand a minimum of five years' experience as a successful classroom teacher. Many ask for at least seven years' teaching and middle management experience.

My experience in secondary schools over the last twenty years is that colleagues take between seven and twelve years to get into a senior management position. The average age range for a senior management appointment in secondary school has been between 33 and 40. In primary schools, teachers can become deputy headteachers in their late twenties and headteachers in their early thirties. However, some people do get into SMT jobs in their late twenties in some secondary schools. I would suggest that it is overarching ambition or incredible impact that takes them there so young. Most colleagues I know, who have been appointed to the SMT, have about ten years' experience under their belt, although I have detected a trend in inner-city schools for dynamic younger candidates to get assistant headships in much less time. The one compelling skill that they have all demonstrated is being good at crowd control with challenging pupils. Although it is undoubtedly an asset for all senior managers to command a presence with pupils, it is only one of many skills needed to do the job well.

In my opinion, you are ready to think of applying for senior management when you have at least three' years middle management experience and have led a team of teachers through a range of situations, leaving a 'mark of improvement' on the way they work. But you increase your likelihood of getting into the SMT if you consider the other important criteria for getting shortlisted for a senior post. These criteria are discussed below under the following headings: Knowledge of educational issues; Getting a further qualification in education; Showing that you have experience of planning, implementing and evaluating at middle management level; Getting a taste of whole-school management experience; and Working out your own educational vision and measuring everything you do against it.

Knowledge of educational issues

A competent and convincing candidate for senior management will have significant knowledge and opinions about all the big educational issues of the day, even if they are not necessarily applying for a job that demands a detailed appreciation of every one of them.

One thing to comfort yourself with as you try for senior management is that the central issues don't change, even though the initiatives to address those issues do. Over the last thirty years, the key issues could perhaps be grouped as follows:

- improving the exam results and the basic quality of education of the school population;
- thinking about whether the way education is organised and qualifications are structured is the most effective way to get the best out of youngsters;
- managing the behaviour and motivation of all pupils better, but particularly those disadvantaged by their home background or 'negative stereotyping' about their race, gender or social class;
- trying to get education and social services to work more effectively together to solve some vulnerable young people's complex problems.

The initiatives around these issues have become increasingly government led and controlled. The Ofsted inspection system aims to ensure that schools and local authorities do not avoid the priorities of central government. As governments come and go, so the political emphasis on tackling the key issues change and initiatives see-saw from one educational dogma to another. As an aspiring senior manager you need to keep up with this debate and keep your eye on all the new educational initiatives, measuring them against your own set of beliefs and practical experience about what does and doesn't work in schools.

At the moment, the initiatives are focused on the following areas:

- changes to the post-14–19 curriculum and proposals for major reform to GCSE and A level. The issue of alternative vocational qualifications is also in the spotlight;
- changes to the way that higher education is funded;
- issues around the 'inclusion' of physically disabled youngsters and emotionally challenging pupils in the mainstream, rather than in special schools;
- drives on improving literacy and numeracy levels through high-profile government initiatives aimed at 11- to 13-year-olds;
- schools taking on a subject specialism and some inner-city schools being converted into 'academies' through public/private funding, with new state-of-the-art buildings and the promise of a more flexible curriculum;
- different learning styles being integrated into pupil schemes of work;
- measuring pupil progress, using value-added data.

These initiatives are currently paramount, but there are many others I have not mentioned and the sheer scale of change planned for any particular moment in the educational world could make you slightly anxious about becoming a member of a senior management team responsible for making sense of it all. One of your biggest challenges when in a senior post is to prioritise what is useful and sensible from the conveyor belt of continuous and confusing changes being suggested. We will return to this in the chapter on building relations with local authorities and central government.

Getting information on educational issues

The best of the current information is drip-fed to you every week in the *Times Educational Supplement*. Other good sources of information are the *Guardian* and the *Independent* education pages and the teaching union magazines. Little more than a half hour flick through the *Times Educational Supplement* every week (not just the job pages) will set you up well. Following up by reading educational books that go into the topic more deeply is also useful from time to time. Some teachers never read a book on educational theory or practice after leaving teacher-training college, which doesn't say a lot for their genuine interest in some important research and reflection from other practitioners.

Obviously, some senior management job applications need expert knowledge on matters such as inclusion, special needs or post-16 education and you would need to read recent government policy papers very thoroughly.

Getting a further qualification in education

If you decide to do a higher degree, such as an education master's, then many potential school employers would see this as an overt sign of your dedication to making yourself knowledgeable about educational issues.

Most universities, including the Open University, offer master's in educational management. To complete one successfully you have to read around the important issues relating to curriculum reform and school improvement in this country. Many master's include modules that require you to put theory into practice by setting up some action research in your own school around some aspect of curriculum improvement. This is a very practical way of rolling up your sleeves and getting direct experience of a whole-school project, so vital for successful senior management job applications.

When I did my master's degree in curriculum management as head of sixth form, I wrote a project on the plans I had drawn up to improve the academic ethos and staying-on rate in that school, post sixteen. The first part of the project charted the way we broadened the curriculum offer in the sixth form to include more vocational qualifications. The second issue revolved around working through an action plan to foster a stronger relationship with the Year 11 parents and market our school sixth form as a better alternative than local FE providers. It helped focus me on the complexities of handling a major school initiative successfully and definitely gave me a strong talking point for my next interview as a senior teacher, two years later.

Showing that you have experience of planning, implementing and evaluating at middle management level

Even if you haven't done a further qualification to broaden your knowledge of educational issues, schools will want to see that you have been able to follow through a curriculum initiative at department level.

Most schools will be expecting you to be able to talk about aspects of your existing work with clarity and enthusiasm. Within that, they will want you to show how you have analysed a problem, planned a solution and worked with a team of teachers to carry out the plan. Most importantly, how honest and analytical are you at reflecting on the success and failure of what you had set out to achieve? These vital skills and experience are just as essential at senior management level on the bigger whole-school stage.

Here is a sample of possible initiatives that would make a good example of past work.

For heads of year

Possible initiatives include:

- implementing an effective personal social education programme which your tutors feel confident to teach and involving outside agencies as guests in its delivery;
- establishing a regular programme for tutor groups to take it in turn to lead assemblies;
- setting up meetings with important child welfare agencies to monitor and support vulnerable pupils in your year group;
- introducing a system of academic monitoring for your year group and selecting an underachieving group of pupils to provide extra support to.

For heads of department and subject co-ordinators

Possible initiatives include:

- a plan to raise the GCSE results in your curriculum area;
- devising a series of assessment pieces to monitor pupil progress in a particular year group in your subject;
- creating a staff rota for supporting teachers with difficult classes, by having a member of staff in the department available to receive a badly behaved pupil from another teacher's lesson at any time of day;
- establishing an extra-curricular programme of clubs in your subject;
- setting up cross-curricular links with other subjects at one of the Key Stages;
- rewriting schemes of work to include practical teaching techniques and materials on different learning styles;
- putting together a programme of peer observation in your subject area, so that teachers can watch each other teach and learn from each other's good practice.

The key to any of these activities for a job application is that you can talk self-reflectively about the challenges you faced and how you rose to them. In the written part of your application, the supporting statement, you would concentrate on highlighting the successes of your work. But at interview you are expected to analyse these achievements and reflect thoughtfully on what worked and what didn't. Interviewers are often more interested in the things that went wrong and how you learnt from them.

Getting a taste of whole-school management experience

It's desirable, though not always essential, to gain some experience of actual strategic whole-school management of the kind you will be asked to do as a senior manager.

If it isn't going to be obtained by doing an action-research project as part of a master's degree in educational management, it can be done on a voluntary basis by shadowing a senior manager or by asking to be given a temporary responsibility for a whole-school process, either on a voluntary basis or, better still, on a paid arrangement as an acting post. Obvious examples that would make you invaluable as an extra pair of hands in your school could be:

- helping with timetabling;
- conducting a project around the effectiveness of student target-setting;
- evaluation of out of hours provision in the school;
- the creation of a student group looking at study skills or learning styles across the curriculum;
- a research project working with a pilot group of parents looking at homework;
- researching new qualifications for the 14–19 curriculum and reporting back to the head and the SMT on their appropriateness for the school;
- offering to run a whole-school training session on a teaching theme that you are very enthusiastic about;
- volunteering to lead on a new government initiative that you know is coming on-stream and might become the remit of an already hard-pressed member of the existing senior management team.

Most schools, whatever their type of intake, have room for a sensible proactive person, who wants to take a lead on some aspect of school life and make a contribution to it. I have been continually amazed, in the seven secondary schools I have now worked in, at just how quickly your colleagues assume you to be an expert about something, almost as soon as you have taken it over. In my middle and senior management posts I have been accepted as a so-called expert on careers education, work experience, special needs, timetabling and option choices, data analysis, assessment and literacy recovery within a couple of weeks of heading them up.

Using your appraisal to get the experience and training you need

If you need to gain experience of a practical variety or a further qualification, you should use the appraisal process to ask for what you want.

An appraisal interview should be more than your school setting you targets. It is also a chance for you to say what you need from your headteacher to get ready for your next career step. This is where you could ask for a voluntary or paid temporary whole-school management experience or some funding and time for a further educational management qualification.

Working out your own educational vision and measuring everything you do against it

You will know when you are ready for senior management when the combination of your experience as a classroom teacher, middle manager and 'human being' helps you construct your own guiding principles about the part you want to play in the life of a school. Mine have increasingly centred around a search for new solutions to old problems. My method of going about it has usually been to probe a problem as deeply and honestly as possible, and to find out what the real sticking point is. I have done this with special needs provision and more recently with the way I have presented pupil data to the staff as a way of improving exam results. As a set of principles it influences the way I lead other teachers on any aspect of school life. You need something personally important to hold onto, when all around you absurd targets are being set and unrealistic policies are being forced down from on high. Having your own core educational values is vital because, as a senior manager, you will often have to be cunning at adapting ill-thought-out school or government initiatives so that you can give them some meaning and impact. There will be more about constructively 'subverting' other people's grand plans and designs in later chapters.

Chapter 2

Applying for the job

In this chapter we look at:

- the differences between assistant and deputy headteacher roles;
- the pros and cons of applying for promotion externally or internally;
- using the school performance tables as a quick way of deciding whether to send for the job details;
- how to use person specifications and job descriptions;
- filling in the application form and crafting a supporting statement;
- preparing for the interview process, in particular the most regular questions that are asked of prospective senior managers;
- anecdotal advice about what to avoid doing at senior management interviews.

Assistant headteacher or deputy headteacher – differences and similarities

These are the two generic job titles in senior management teams (SMTs), other than the headteacher: one is described as 'assistant' and the other as 'deputy'.

Assistant headteacher and deputy headteacher can mean very different job descriptions in different schools. Despite the huge variation, certain characteristics of the positions often hold good and need careful consideration. At present, both positions are paid on a leadership scale and are not subject to the same employment conditions as other teachers. Whereas ordinary teachers are contracted to work 1,265 hours a year on teaching lessons or attending other meetings, there is no time limit for those on the leadership grade. They are expected to carry out anything that the headteacher can reasonably ask of them. This usually includes doing break, lunch and after-school duties on a regular basis and getting involved in all aspects of the running of the school. For example, the leadership team will not be guaranteed the same immunity of invigilation from public exams, when the Workforce Remodelling Agreement comes into play in 2006.

In a primary school, the pay differential between a teacher on the highest point of their pay spine with additional management points and that of a deputy headteacher on a low leadership point may be small. Before you go on to the leadership scale you should consider whether the extra work you may be asked to do is worth a potentially marginal financial reward.

Assistant headteacher

- This is usually the first post in senior management.
- It is the replacement for the term 'senior teacher', although in some schools assistant headteachers replaced the role of the deputy headteacher as well.
- It is usually a more junior position in a secondary school management team where there are one or more deputy headteachers.
- It is paid at a lower level on the leadership scale than most deputy headteachers.
- It is often an enhanced middle management position: for example, a head of department or head of year, with an important whole-school responsibility 'bolted on' the end.
- Heads of sixth form or overall heads of Key Stage Three (Years 7–9) or Key Stage Four (10 and 11) can be put on at this level. In a small secondary school, the Key Stage co-ordinators may have no other heads of year under them.
- The assistant headteacher may have an entirely cross-curricular responsibility, such as the special needs or information technology co-ordinator. In recent times this has included high-profile whole-school initiatives such as specialist schools

manager. In the 1980s the same level of responsibility might have been given to the school manager of TVEI (Technical Vocational Educational Initiative). Titles will come and go, as will initiatives, but at this level you are likely to be asked to manage some kind of whole-school project in addition to your middle management responsibilities;

- Some assistant headteacher posts are described as 'free-standing.' This implies that there is no middle management role and only a cocktail of whole-school responsibilities. It is these types of assistant headship that are most similar to the deputy headteacher positions.
- Assistant headteachers are often differentiated from deputy headteachers by having at least a 50 per cent teaching timetable or more, leaving much less time to carry out their whole-school responsibilities.

Deputy headteacher

Deputy headteachers usually carry out whole-school responsibilities only. This can be divided into curriculum or pastoral deputy headships. The former manages the construction of the timetable, assessment, reporting and teaching/learning across the whole school. The latter oversees the work of year heads, the learning support services, mentors and non-teaching staff.

Fashions for deputy headteacher job descriptions change with each decade. At present it is very common for any variety of combination of the above pastoral and curriculum roles to fall under one person's remit. Combinations can include line management of several heads of year, the supervision of the work of a number of big departments along with a major cross-curricular initiative such as the Key Stage Three Strategy on Literacy. These roles often rotate in the team on a two- or three-year basis, to broaden every deputy headteacher's experience. Some deputy headteachers will be in charge of a whole upper or lower school building if a school is on a split site.

In some instances, each of the above are divided up and given to a large team of assistant headteachers, who report directly to the one deputy headteacher in the school.

Deputy headteachers normally have teaching loads of between 25 and 50 per cent, leaving time for these heavier whole-school responsibilities.

Primary schools

Most primary schools have only one deputy headteacher, and the real issue for them is whether they are expected to teach a class all day and do management duties after school. There is a variety of working conditions, but many primary school deputies get at least 50 per cent non-contact time.

In a very real sense, the primary deputy would deputise for the headteacher if he or she were away. In a large secondary school, many of the assistant headteachers and deputy headteachers would not be the first in line to run the school in the absence of the headteacher.

Confusion and lack of clarity over roles

What is clear is that the formal titles of assistant and deputy headteacher do not always define who is a junior and who is a senior member of the senior management team. In one school an assistant headteacher will perform the job description of a deputy headteacher. In another school the senior team is only assistant headteachers and elsewhere, only deputies.

However, the majority of aspiring senior managers will first cross the line to assistant headteacher and then climb to deputy headship. Few assistant headteachers will rise straight to headship, but, in theory, with a large strategic job description, the jump is possible. Nor is it impossible to go straight from middle manager to deputy headteacher role, skipping out assistant headship completely.

When in doubt, look at the pay scale. If the school is offering a high salary range on the leadership scale, way above what you are paid as a middle manager, it is probably looking for someone described as an assistant headteacher and already on the leadership scale to move up to the deputy headteacher position.

Making the decision to apply for a senior management team position

It is as big a jump going from head of subject to assistant/deputy headteacher as it was to go from ordinary class teacher to middle management. For some teachers it will happen just by waiting in their own school for an internal promotion. But most people will not be in the right place at the right time and will have to cast their net wider.

Making an internal application to the SMT

You should think long and hard before making any internal application for a job that you are not absolutely guaranteed getting. Setting yourself up for a promotion in your current workplace and then failing to get it usually leaves a bitter taste in the mouth. Despite the plethora of statements schools have about equal opportunities and fair selection processes, there is always a hidden agenda. You might not get a post you would obtain externally for any of the following reasons:

- Your past reputation in the school means you are not part of the in-crowd of courtiers surrounding a headteacher.
- Your school needs you in your current role so badly that you would not be easy to replace if you were to be promoted internally.
- Somebody else has been groomed 'in house' for the SMT job already.
- Your school is actively trying to move you on.
- There's another good internal candidate in the school with a better profile for the job than you.
- There's a good external candidate offering a range of skills and experiences that the headteacher feels the school is in desperate need of.
- The headteacher wants to appoint someone with fresh ideas from outside.
- The headteacher wants to bring in someone he has worked well with before.

It is common for external assistant headteachers to be appointed because they can offer half a week's teaching in a shortage subject or maybe bolster up a weak department, not because they were the best candidate for the whole-school aspects of the job description.

Why internal applications are often more problematic than external applications

In some cases, being the internal candidate works in your favour and you get offered the job because the school really doesn't want to lose you. But making an external application is less emotionally charged if you are not selected.

When you apply externally for a job and don't get it, you walk away from the scene of battle, dust yourself down and live to fight another day. When you fail to get an internal SMT post, you have to go on working with the same headteacher and the successful candidate. The temptation to feel disenchanted is strong. This is not a good basis for a happy and motivated working life nor the positive psychological foundation from which to apply externally.

Preparing external applications

Responding to job adverts and sending for details

Before wasting your time sending for the details of a job, a tiny bit of research and soul-searching can help.

Keep a copy of the school league tables when they come out in the national newspapers in the winter. They may not be much help for parents in choosing their children's school, but they are great for a quick analysis of whether you would choose to teach there. The most pertinent piece of data in secondary schools is the percentage of pupils getting five A to C grades at GCSE. For primary schools, the end of Key Stage Two SATs tell you a lot. This is a much quicker way of ruling out unsuitable schools than all the glossy brochures and mission statements that you are bombarded with when you get the application pack.

I have used the percentage of five A to C grades as my most accurate predictor of whether a school had a bottom-ended socio-economic pupil intake and might be too wild for me to cope with as a senior manager. But results could also tell me if a school was so academic that it might be too 'stuck up' to short-list a person like me, with lots of inner-city experience.

Now that most secondary schools are doing vocational qualifications that have boosted their five A to C equivalent results, you have to be canny about reading between the lines. A school that used to have 25 per cent of pupils with five A to C with ordinary GCSE may now have 60 per cent of pupils with five A to C equivalents, with vocational exams worth up to four GCSEs in one subject. These qualifications are usually easier to get and the underlyingly challenging student population is probably much the same. Look out for any massive rises in results and be suspicious of them.

I have always had my own personal boundaries when I applied for senior team jobs. However, if you want SMT experience at any cost, then just apply for anything that moves in the geographical vicinity you want to be. If you want to cross over from inner-city to top-notch suburban school, then you'll have to think very carefully about how to make your recent skills and experience relevant to the other side of the street. Likewise, in the other direction.

Getting the job application pack

Wedged in between all the kite marks for quality and excellence in this or that subject, the school development plan, last Ofsted report and school magazine, you will find the most important documents – the person specification and the job description for the senior post you are looking at.

Person specification

The kind of personality traits and generic skills the successful applicant should possess are usually summed up by the person specification of your future employer. Below is a typical list of strengths asked for. They can be organised in three categories: communication and leadership; personal ambition and drive; and your personal belief system.

HOW WELL YOU COMMUNICATE AND LEAD

- a good teacher;
- good interpersonal skills with staff;
- ability to communicate effectively with other stakeholders, such as the local authority, governors and local community;
- good at leading teams of teachers;
- effective working within a team, such as the SMT;
- experience of successfully carrying out a curriculum reform or a whole-school initiative and then evaluating it;
- a strong presence with pupils;
- sense of humour and ability to work under pressure to meet deadlines

YOUR PERSONAL AMBITION AND DRIVE

- evidence of further professional training to improve communication and organisation skills and knowledge base;
- ambitious, intending to move up to headship;

WHAT YOU BELIEVE IN

- an educationalist with a strong vision of how to improve teaching and learning;
- an ability to turn that vision into practice;
- a strong commitment to the inclusion of different types of pupils in a school and an understanding of equal opportunities issues around race, gender and class.

These personal skills come up again and again, even though senior team job descriptions vary greatly.

Job description

Here is a typical sample of job definitions for assistant headteachers from the *Times Educational Supplement*.

- teaching and learning
- learning support
- student services
- pupil performance
- curriculum enhancement
- extension and out of hours learning activities
- performance data
- marketing and external relations
- PSHE
- community
- communications.

Some of these job definitions seem easy to understand, but others contain a strange mix of specific responsibilities, grouped under pompous titles like curriculum enhancement, teaching and learning or pupil performance. They sound like the natural strategic remit of any headteacher worth their salt. Yet they often appear to be delegated to a senior manager on the lower tier of the SMT. A closer inspection of the job details of a teaching and learning leadership role reveals a remit of working on student data analysis. You might have been the sort of person who wanted to help train teachers in classroom strategies as part of your teaching and learning responsibility and when the revealed purpose of the assistant headteacher's job becomes clear, analysing pupil data might not appeal. It's vital to check the exact job description in the application pack. The devil is always lurking in the detail. But checking it is not always that easy when at least half the job specifications resort to a 'cover all' clause: 'Responsibilities will be negotiated around the strengths of the successful candidate'; or 'A new structure within the school leadership group is possible and therefore the responsibilities of the post are negotiable.'

Schools always declare that getting the best possible candidate is their priority. This means that demonstrating the personal skills specified by the person specifications in the application pack becomes more important than trying to fit your previous experience into the job description being outlined. As we shall see later in this chapter, you need to produce a carefully constructed covering letter or supporting statement that addresses both person specification and job description.

Filling in the application form and writing a supporting statement

Dealing with the application forms

It often takes a campaign of many applications to get your first senior management position. So it is important to get the filling out of 'standard' application forms down to a fine art. The first thing to appreciate is that there isn't such a thing as a standard application form. Local authorities and sometimes individual schools have devised their own version of the same thing. All of them lack space to fill in the information in one or more of the boxes. For example, I have now worked in about seven schools over twenty years, but there is never enough room in the employment history box.

To make more of the inadequate space that is given, I draw very faint pencil lines which are narrow enough for me to jam in all the jobs that I have had. Then I rub them out. When you can, it is far better to download the application form and type in your information, as you can easily extend the boxes if you need to. But at the time of writing this book, this opportunity is not always available and is sometimes so fraught with technical glitches, it still remains best to do it the old-fashioned way.

The only bit of the form that I have always typed and not handwritten is the covering letter or supporting statement. It is simply too long and detailed to rely on keeping handwriting neat and tidy, so I attach it to the application form.

The question that you are invariably asked to address in the supporting statement is: 'Describe how your past experience and skills make you suitable for the post.' To do this effectively, you have to ask some searching questions about yourself, your own personality and career experiences to date. Going through the headings in Chapter 1 and asking yourself the following questions will help you do this:

- Do I have the knowledge of educational issues I need?
- Do I need to broaden my knowledge with a further educational qualification?
- Can I show how I have been a successful middle manager?
- Could I get a taste of whole-school leadership experience before I apply for a senior position?
- What is my educational vision and how best can I explain it to others?

The supporting statement

The supporting statement is at the heart of your written application for a senior management job in a school. It's sometimes called a covering letter, in which case it is addressed to a named person and signed off with a 'yours sincerely'.

For each application that you make, you should modify the emphasis of what you say about yourself according to the job description and person specification being suggested. What you choose to highlight in more detail may also vary according to whether you are applying for an inner-city, leafy suburban or very high achieving grammar school. Different aspects of your past experience may interest your audience and a fresh slant on your skills and qualities may readily catch their eye. Whatever the situation, all good applications will find a way of stressing your personal qualities and strengths.

Below is a supporting statement for an assistant headteacher's post in a London inner-city comprehensive school. All the information in this sample is fictitious. The candidate, Tina Watson, has ten years' experience in three secondary schools in London. In the first school, Ruddlesfield, she taught history before being promoted to head of careers. After four years, she left to become head of sixth form at Grove Wood School. After three years in this position, she went into a senior middle management post as head of the humanities faculty and gifted/talented pupil co-ordinator at Selbury Manor School. The first and the third schools are challenging, mixed, inner-city comprehensives and the second school is a suburban school. The post she is applying for is as assistant headteacher, with job description to be negotiated according to the strengths of the candidate. The teaching commitment is 55 per cent of the week. The school has a mixed inner-city intake.

I would like to be considered for the post of assistant headteacher at . . .

SECTION ONE – MANAGEMENT AND TEACHING EXPERIENCE

I have a wide range of experience and qualifications, having worked in varying middle managements posts in three schools over the last ten years. This has given me deep and wide-ranging experience of many key educational issues.

In my current school I am responsible for the Humanities Faculty, consisting of religious studies, history, geography and citizenship. I hold a further whole-school responsibility as Gifted and Talented Pupils Co-ordinator, a major strand of the Excellence in Cities Initiative. In my first school I led cross-curricular, whole-school initiatives on Careers Education and School–Industry Links. At Grove Wood Community School I was the Head of Sixth Form, responsible for 180 students. This rich variety of pastoral and curriculum experience has helped shape my principal educational views. In particular, the importance of 'positive discipline' in all types of school, the need for detailed curriculum planning and the necessity of establishing close teacher teamwork in which goals are set and regularly monitored.

I am an experienced and successful classroom teacher, having taught history (to A-level) and religious studies (to GCSE) in a wide variety of settings, two of which would be categorised as challenging multcultural, inner-city schools. My pupils' exam results have been well above the school average.

I have sound knowledge of current educational issues, in particular those relating to school improvement and the concept of 'value added' as a way of measuring such improvement. As a teacher and a manager I am particularly interested in the issue of improving teaching, especially in groups where poor behaviour and low motivation are the 'norms' throughout the day. I am currently engaged in an action-research project at Selbury Manor with Year 9, doing a pupil and teacher survey of the types of teaching strategies that work best in challenging groups.

SECTION TWO – MANAGEMENT SKILLS AND ATTITUDES (TEAM LEADERSHIP, STAFF DEVELOPMENT, IMPLEMENTING CHANGE SUCCESSFULLY THROUGH EFFECTIVE DECISION-MAKING)

The successful implementation of whole-school initiatives is inevitably very challenging for staff. In my rich variety of pastoral and curriculum leadership roles I have always worked to plan and implement positive change. As Careers Co-ordinator I established a flourishing careers education programme, which was delivered by school tutors in PSHE time. As Head of Sixth Form I introduced vocational courses and encouraged teachers to respond to the new teaching methodology that they required. I introduced all sixth form students to Individual Action Planning and target-setting so that could take increasing responsibility for their own learning. Currently as Head of Faculty at Selbury Manor, I have effected major curriculum change in three National Curriculum subjects, line-managing a radical overhaul to schemes of work, teaching and assessment methods. My additional role as Gifted and Talented Co-ordinator means I lead a cross-curricular team of project managers within the school as well as working in a team of five local secondary schools on joint projects for our area of East London.

My ability to lead teams of colleagues effectively and communicate to the whole staff convincingly has been an essential ingredient for success. I have had to learn how to delegate and how to action plan carefully. Each situation has been very different but as a leader I always work on the principle of setting clear priorities for the team and building on my colleagues' strengths and enthusiasms, encouraging them to give of their very best. In my current position as Gifted and Talented Pupil Co-ordinator, this means managing a diverse team of teachers with a wide range of subject disciplines.

Through consistent monitoring and positive encouragement of staff, I have initiated significant improvements in curriculum delivery and the quality of learning. In all three of my management posts, the key to implementing successful change has been clear planning, sensible collaboration and teamwork, and above all, my high expectations of colleagues as their team leader. Currently as Head of a Humanities Faculty with eight members, I need good writing and oral skills mixed with endless energy, adaptability and optimism. I have learned to expect the 'unexpected' as a daily occurrence and deal with it with as much 'poise' and purpose as is humanly possible. This has demanded resilience, flexibility and a well-developed sense of humour. To function effectively at this level I have acquired a variety of IT skills.

SECTION THREE – EDUCATIONAL VISION AND PHILOSOPHY

Underpinning my education vision is a firm commitment to equal opportunities. As a teacher and as a manager, I have a practical daily commitment to challenging 'stereotypes' about race and gender that can lead students into narrowing their range of choices in life and underestimating what they are capable of achieving. This has formed a daily part of my effort to raise the quality of the learning experience for all the students in their Humanities lessons at Selbury Manor. It was at the heart of the careers programme I devised at Ruddlesfield and the action planning I introduced into the sixth form at Grove Park School.

I firmly believe that with clarity of purpose and incisive strategic planning all schools can make significant improvements for their pupils, whatever their starting point. The key to success is mobilising all the staff into a team that is working consistently towards clear goals of school improvement, within a management structure that sets firm expectations on who is accountable for each step towards that positive change.

CONCLUSION

I believe my knowledge, understanding and experience of leading, managing and innovating over the last ten years in schools make me a versatile and effective school leader. My present headteacher, Peter Brown, has given me a lot of encouragement and support in my ambition to obtain a senior leadership role. To this end, I have set about completing a Master's in Education Management and have also enrolled at the initial entry stage of the NPQH (National professional headteacher qualification).

Observations about the sample supporting statement

I have constructed similar supporting statements to this one to get three positions in senior management, using my own personal mix of experiences. I have also seen colleagues' statements that have got them shortlisted successfully. If you have a good relationship with somebody somewhere in senior management, it's really helpful to see as many varieties of supporting statement as you can, before you write your own.

From what I have observed, there are two approaches to writing a supporting statement. The first follows the person criteria point by point, showing how you meet it. The second makes reference to the person specification but does not follow each point on it laboriously. In fact, it accepts that in giving certain examples from your past experiences you imply certain character traits such as initiative, determination and good communication skills. The example I have given in this chapter follows the second model. The great advantage of this approach for the supporting statement is that you can make it flow, so it becomes a decent piece of writing, which is crisp and entertaining to read. Statements that follow person criteria slavishly tend to have repetitive, overlapping paragraphs. A statement needs to draw a reader in, rather than repel them with boring repeats or disjointed information. Your letter may need to stand out from another thirty written applications. Give it a strong personal feeling so that it does just that.

No one style of supporting statement will always get you shortlisted. You could spend hours on a statement and produce the perfect specimen but still be rejected because the selection process has hidden selection criteria you will never find out about. Maybe they don't think your experience in middle management is long enough. Perhaps they are only going through the motions of getting an external field and have a strong internal candidate they want to appoint. There are whole hosts of reasons to stop you being shortlisted, but the key to success is to have prepared a basic statement that usually works. If you have had an application rejected at the written stage you can try and phone a school to ask why. Most headteachers will give you some kind of feedback after the appointment process is over. Sometimes they can point out very useful things you have missed out from your supporting statement, but at other times they will make up things to justify a poor decision on their part or obscure the hidden agenda for selection. You shouldn't waste your time looking for this kind of feedback unless your statement hardly ever gets you shortlisted.

Adapting statements for different job applications

Some lucky teachers get into senior management on their first or second attempt. Most people have to try many more times than that to get through. So you should aim to have a supporting statement that often gets you shortlisted, which you can adapt slightly for each job application. Such a piece of writing will only need some paragraphs altered to make them pertinent to the individual school or a particular job description. But the core of the statement holds onto your educational vision and your personality strengths, giving off that strong flavour of 'you' each time.

For example, I added an additional paragraph for a church secondary school I applied for. It would have gone in to this sample statement just above my educational vision on equal opportunities. 'I am sure I could support the Christian identity of your School. My first School, Ruddlesfield, was also a Church of England School and I was able to make a direct contribution to its spiritual ethos by taking regular assemblies.'

Good points about the sample statement

- Tina has made the most of her experience in three schools in three very different middle management experiences.
- She has stressed the whole-school, cross-curricular nature of her first management experience as head of careers and of her current additional role as gifted and talented pupil co-ordinator.
- Her current management role is very curriculum orientated and her last one as a head of sixth form has a pastoral flavour. This is an impressive combination of roles.
- She shows you that she is first and foremost an enthusiastic teacher.
- She gives examples of important school improvement themes she is currently involved in as head of humanities and has previously been responsible for as head of sixth form.

- She links what she has done in with her own personal educational and management philosophy. You get a strong flavour of what she thinks is important in schools. She addresses the vital issue of her personal style for leading and motivating a team of teachers.
- She stresses personal strengths that will fit in well with a senior management team position.
- There is a very clear statement of educational vision, linking it to the social inclusion and equal opportunities themes, which are found on almost all person specifications for senior school jobs.
- The use of sub-headings to group information can be very eye-catching for the reader. It is often a clever way to regroup the points in the person specification in an order which you feel more comfortable to write about, cutting out unnecessary overlap in a long person specification list.
- The statement has a sense of direction about it, with one paragraph flowing on from another. There is a strong sense of 'character' in her writing. Hopefully, this 'character' will come out in the interview and get her the job.

Other written assessment

A few schools ask you to jump through another hoop. In addition to filling in their application form and doing a supporting statement, they set you a short written exercise. The most common example is: Describe a curriculum innovation you have led. What was the planned outcome and how did you learn from your experience?

Such exercises plan to see the level of your experience, your writing skills at describing the management of change and your powers to self-reflect honestly. It is almost as though these schools do not trust the supporting statement to bring out these vital personal strengths in their senior management candidate.

I know that schools that make the written application to them very strenuous end up losing good candidates. Getting a busy middle manager to jump through hours of written assessment before they even get the guarantee of an interview may be unwise.

The first application form and supporting statement you make for senior positions will take many hours to prepare. Subsequent applications are much quicker if you store everything you have done before on a computer. Nevertheless, making a new application takes at least two hours tweaking time on the supporting statement and a further two hours to fill out a new school or local authority application form.

The interview process

Your written application and your well-oiled supporting statement get you through the door of the school you want a job at. Once through that door, what you have said in your application and how well you have said it count for very little. You are now judged on your interview performance alone.

The education world always likes to complicate rather than simplify the assessment of prospective senior management candidates. The interview process usually includes some or all the following:

- interview with the headteacher and another senior manager or the chair of governors;
- interview with a separate governors' panel;
- interview with an LEA representative like a school link inspector;
- interview with a group of pupils from the school council;
- teaching a lesson (prospective assistant headteachers rather than deputy headteachers are asked to do this at secondary school, where their teaching load is likely to be 50 per cent or more;
- group role play exercises;
- written exercises.

Some interview processes last for a day but the majority spin out over two, as they also include a guided tour of the school. The field of candidates is sometimes shortened for the second day although many schools take all four or five candidates through to a final selection procedure, which usually consists of an oral presentation and a final interview.

Oral presentation

This is a short presentation of between five and ten minutes to the final interview panel. The title for this is sometimes given to you over the phone the night before if you are taken through to the final shortlist. At other times you are asked to come in for the final interview, where a topic for presentation is given to you on the spot with about thirty minutes' preparation time. Whichever the favoured method, you are likely to be faced with very predictable topics: Describe how you would raise academic achievement in the short and medium term at the new school; What do you see as the key issues facing the new school as the assistant headteacher in charge of . . . ? How would you plan to tackle these issues?

Group role play

These are becoming common, as interview panels try and find ever more sophisticated ways of working out personal qualities in their candidates. They were first used at headship interviews, but now the practice is spreading down the professional chain.

The Goldfish Bowl is the most frequently used. The interview panel watch you discuss an issue with the other job candidates and come up with a group solution. They are watching to see if you have a dominant or passive style, generate good ideas to move the discussion forward and are inclusive of other team members. The Goldfish Bowl exercise is a window on your oral communication skills and how you might apply them to leading a team. To do as well as possible, you must engage positively with the exercise and suspend disbelief by acting as though you are genuinely working in a hastily constituted senior management team, not just competing against your job rivals. The basic ground rule is not to show off or try and upstage anybody else. To impress your judges, you must see being in the fish bowl as a collaborative exercise. Try and show the assessors at least one example of the following qualities:

- taking a lead on moving the discussion on;
- listening to others in the group and feeding back their viewpoints positively;
- asking probing questions of the issues being discussed;
- contributing to the summary of the group position.

Goldfish Bowl exercises do put you under the spotlight in an artificial way. The topic for discussion may be one you feel enthusiastic or ambivalent about. For example, I was asked to discuss the benefits of a school's successful bid for language school status. Having just spoken to a selection of pupils, I felt the school had made an error of judgement in selecting this specialist status. It was not surprising when my contribution to the Goldfish Bowl discussion was judged too negative.

From a personal viewpoint, group role play exercises make the whole interview process more interesting as you get a chance to assess the qualities of your competitors and learn from their strengths and weaknesses. It is the only part of the selection procedure not conducted behind closed doors.

Written exercises

The written exercises are similar to the ones some schools ask you do before you get an interview. Clearly, it is vital for a senior manager to write as well as speak effectively.

Favourites at this stage include the pre-interview ones that I have already mentioned along with tasks such as these:

- a letter to a parent regarding some kind of complaint;
- analysis of pupil data from a government report. You are asked to comment on the trends it shows on pupil attainment in the school and devise an action plan to address your findings;
- deputy headteachers are often asked to do an in-tray exercise in which they are asked to prioritise how they would respond to a series of urgent demands on their time.

The final interview

This is usually in front of a very large group of all the people you may have already seen in panels from the previous day with a few extra governors included. It is not unknown for the panel to have as many as twelve people on it. It feels like being up on a court martial or waiting for the firing squad.

Typical interview questions

The one thing you can guess with 90 per cent accuracy is the range of interview questions you'll be asked for an SMT job. Given their probability, it makes sense to write them down and prepare notes or bullet points with your answers. Go through them in your head or even out loud as you drive or walk to work. Practice makes you much better, if not perfect at answering them. However, there is a fine balance between being well rehearsed and still being able to think on your feet. You can second guess the vast majority of the interview questions but not all of them, so if you over-prepare a script, you might not be in the right frame of mind to use the adrenalin factor to ad-lib enthusiastically when you need to. You don't want to sound like a robot, reeling out your word-perfect answers. The interview process is not about remembering all your lines perfectly but creating a positive impression. Part of that is spontaneity and 'off the cuff' thoughtfulness.

Body language

Apparently, at least 90 per cent of our communication is not what we say but how we carry ourselves physically, as we say it. I would suggest to you that your body language will look as confident as it can be if you have rehearsed your answers well.

Most frequently asked questions for senior management interviews

I have subdivided the likely questions under four broad headings. As always, there is some overlap between them. The first are questions about your personality and motivations. The other groups are 'how would you do this' questions on curriculum, pupils, parents and staff.

About you as a person

- Why do you want to come to this school as deputy/assistant headteacher?
- What do you see as your personal strengths? Can you give us an example of when you have used them well?
- What are your shortcomings? How do you compensate for them?
- How do you handle stress in the job?
- How do you see your career developing five years from now?
- What further training would you need to undertake to fulfil all aspects of this senior management job description?

- Tell us the most useful things you have learned from your past training experiences?
- What is the difference between 'leadership' and 'management'?

'How would you do this?' questions about the curriculum

- Tell us about a major curriculum initiative that you have seen through successfully.
- Describe what you would do when planning an intervention to improve a weak department.
- What makes a good lesson?
- Tell us about a good lesson you have taught. What would you have changed to make it even better?
- How should we make the best use of pupil assessment data across the school?
- What do you see as the key issues for this kind of school?
- Can you explain how you would uphold our school policy on equal opportunities as a member of the senior team?
- Is 'setting' a better way forward than mixed-ability teaching?
- How do you think the recent government paper (something topical) will impact on student achievement?
- How do you see the role of the deputy headteacher in terms of accountability to the governors?
- Tell us about a recent book or education document you have read. What did you think of it?
- How would you go about leading a whole-school push on literacy?
- How would you go about leading a whole-school plan to raise levels of numeracy?
- What makes a good marking policy. How can a school enforce it effectively?
- How would you raise the profile of homework in this school?
- How would you encourage out-of-school learning and extension activities?
- How would you encourage the use of more information technology across the school?

'How would you do this?' questions about pupils (and their parents)

- How would you raise the profile of the school in the local community?
- What would you do to increase the active participation of parents in school?
- A parent tells you that her daughter is being badly bullied. How would you deal with the situation?
- Other questions on 'how would you handle' difficult parents (homework, classwork, bad behaviour in the lesson, complaining about the behaviour of one of the teachers).
- What makes an effective anti-bullying policy?
- How would you ensure that this school has an effective reporting system to the parents?
- How would you go about introducing a strategy to improve attendance at school and punctuality to lessons?
- How would you make students more accountable for monitoring their own performance?
- What is needed in a good guidance programme for each year group? How should it be delivered?
- Suggest some practical strategies for helping refugee pupils settle in.
- How would you plan to raise achievement in a particularly underperforming ethnic minority group?
- What makes for effective primary–secondary school liaison?
- What practical steps could be take in a school to make inclusion a reality?
- What are the key ingredients of an active policy on social inclusion? What would you see as the practical priorities for such a policy in the pupils' classroom experience?
- What are the principles on which a good behaviour management strategy is based?

'How would you do this?' questions about managing the staff

- What benefits can be gained from performance management interviews?
- How should one go about making best use of all forms of support staff?

- A member of staff comes to you and says that a Year 9 girl has got heavy bruising on her arms and legs. How would you deal with this?
- How have you gone about successful team building in the past?
- What do you do when you have a team player who won't cooperate?

Things that can go wrong at SMT interviews

The moment you walk into the school on interview day, formal and informal selection processes begin. This is true for all levels of teaching appointment, but becomes even more of an issue for assistant, deputy and headteacher interviews, as staff of all types, governors and pupils feed back into the selection process for these high-profile posts. Some have been formally asked to do so, but others will make judgements or observations they feel are important enough to pass on to members of the interview panel anecdotally.

Staff you used to work with

If they have known you or worked with you before, you can be sure they will supply their observations to someone on the panel. People you had good relationships with may help your application, though a recommendation from some trusted allies may not always be that helpful. But those you didn't get on with can be guaranteed to put a real spanner in your works. If they are in the SMT you are trying to join, my experience is you might as well give up and go home.

Controversial opinions expressed at the wrong moments

You need to be careful to moderate your opinions on anything that might be a touchy issue at your interview school. A colleague of mine failed to pick up signals from conversations with the staff, senior team and governors at an 11–16 school that they were obsessed with the recovery of their sixth form provision, lost five years previously. He failed to appreciate that the chair of governors was a leading campaigner to restore the sixth form. Consequently, when he was asked about whether it was important for a school to have 16–18 courses, he advocated making the best of 11–16 status and moving on from the past. This was completely the wrong answer for the chair of governors, and even if other interviewers found it sensible, the chair became implacably opposed to his appointment from that moment.

This example demonstrates that it's important to adopt a safe position, rather than anything too hard line or potentially controversial. You must be sure that your opinion is shared by key members of the panel before you nail your colours to the mast.

Educational opinions expressed in the wrong way

To be successful at an SMT interview, you need to be aware of the varied nature of your audience. Many parent or community governors will not have detailed knowledge of education and curriculum and will be confused if you give educationally technical answers. But the headteacher and the local authority representatives will expect much more sophisticated specialist answers. When you answer a question, think of the diversity of your audience and keep jargon to a minimum. If you want to give an answer to both types of audience make sure you give the more specialist bit at the beginning of the answer but end with a practical re-interpretation that the whole panel can make sense of.

Being caught offguard

You also need to watch what you say and do with all staff in the school, not just the ones involved in the interview process. At one school another teacher I know was told that she had spoken dismissively to the office staff at the end of the day, when asking for directions to the station and that this had been reported to the interview panel. She could barely recall the interchange but did remember that she had felt absolutely exhausted after a gruelling day of interviews and her body language could have been misinterpeted. From the moment you walk in, everything is being watched and analysed. I have found myself needing to guard against remarks or asides that could be taken as too flippant and therefore an example of my lacking the gravitas and high seriousness required for the job. Whatever you think of the pompous absurdities of the educational system, you need to combine caution and confidence during the interview day. When you have actually got the job and know the characters and personalities in your school better, you will know who you can have a joke with and who is likely to take themselves and the job over seriously.

Being light-hearted, relaxed and suitably irreverent about many educational issues can be a useful management quality, as we shall see in Chapter 4, when we look at building effective relationships with staff. During an interview these should be kept to a minimum as they could cost you the job!

Being too honest about your weaknesses

By sitting on a number of senior management interview panels, I have observed that the average interviewers want to appoint a person who can self-reflect honestly on personal weaknesses. But it is important to be fairly selective about what one chooses to highlight 'honestly' as a weakness. One candidate I interviewed blew his chances of a SMT job by saying he had often felt stressed at work. Although his explanation of how he dealt with this stress was utterly convincing and showed real maturity, many panel members felt that he might be too nervous and highly strung to enter the senior team. It is much better to pick out a weakness that could at the same time be seen as a strength. So finding it difficult to delegate because of the high standards you set yourself will go down better than describing how you successfully overcome feelings of frustration and anger in the job.

In another interview, one SMT candidate was brutally honest, saying that he had left a job after only one year because of an unsuccessful love affair with a colleague. The panel affected to be very impressed by his honesty and candour, partly to cover up their own embarrassment, but as soon as he had left the room, they ruled him out completely! His performance had been singularly impressive in all areas, but the over-honest personal disclosure showed a serious lack of judgement to the interview panel.

The point to learn from these examples is that you need to be honest about yourself, but not disconcertingly so.

Answering trick questions and asking silly questions

My current headteacher often asks candidates how they would assemble a flat-packed piece of furniture from IKEA. There is no right answer to this question but the range of responses people give cast interesting light on their personalities. Some people bore the pants off the interview panel by saying how they would lay out every screw and panel meticulously. At the other extreme, one candidate said that he would delegate the job to his wife, an answer that the panel found witty and self-deprecating, but somewhat irresponsible and chauvinistic. But candidates come up with weird answers that can sound warning bells. One woman did not explain how she would put the furniture together, but instead how she would colour code all her shoes, blouses and trousers on the new shelves. As her answer unravelled, so did her chances of getting a job!

You can also be judged adversely by the quality of the questions you ask at the end of an interview. One or two sensible questions about the job or conditions of work make sense, especially when it is information you could not have gleaned from other sources. But beware the one question that demonstrates an obssession with something essentially minor or irrelevant to the core job function. For example, the candidate who only had one question about whether he would have a car parking space reserved for him at the school every morning irritated the appointing headteacher, who was expecting probing questions on a different kind of drive – one to improve literacy levels in the school.

Doing everything right and still being unsuccessful

Sometimes you can give the performance of your life and still not get the job. The same or a lesser performance on another day in a different school will see you successful and the subject of glowing personal accolades.

In the interview process, there are no guarantees. Each school is looking for a different mix of qualities in the person they wish to appoint. Your face might fit, even if you don't perform brilliantly. You could be rejected, even when you are great! The secret of success is to keep the application process going and never give up.

Chapter 3

The first week, the first half term

In this chapter we look at:

- having a proper talk with your new headteacher about the job description before you start;
- creating a stable office space in the first few days and having some meetings in which you look, listen and learn, rather than make decisions on anything;
- not committing yourself to anything until you have a full understanding of its implications;
- getting back to people when you've promised to – start to establish a reputation for 'my word is my bond';
- meeting a few early deadlines from your headteacher to show you are a person who can be relied on to deliver.

Negotiating the job description

After the initial glow of your promotion has worn off and the day of reckoning approaches, you need to start preparing yourself for the new job. Before you can do that properly you need to get into the new school and have a proper conversation with the headteacher. You may have had a snatched conversation about your roles and responsibilities when you were being offered the job, but at such moments of triumph, it's very hard to concentrate on the details.

During the few weeks before you start your new job you need to negotiate what your remit will be. It's important to blend willingness to co-operate with hard-headed realism about not being completely overburdened. Yet when you are new and basking in the glory of being the chosen one, it is all too easy to try and accommodate all requests. I learned that lesson the hard way when I was phoned by my new headteacher a week after my appointment. He asked me to become special needs co-ordinator myself. The published job description had included line managing the whole of the learning support department, including the existing co-ordinator. Despite that, I found myself agreeing to this fundamental change without thinking through the significance of it on my new working day. It was a rash decision, which I should have negotiated and it meant two very challenging years in senior management.

As you discuss your job description, try and include something that you are passionately interested in. For me, it was the two hours on my timetable to run staff training on literacy recovery.

Job descriptions and primary schools

In a primary school, as the sole deputy, it's even more important to negotiate a job description because everything and anything could come your way as the headteacher's only other senior manager. Given that you may have a lot of teaching as a primary deputy, it's important that your non-contact time is part of the deal for certain time-consuming projects.

What is absolutely clear is that before you arrive for your first day in your new school you need to have a properly worked out job description. Whether primary or secondary, you should make sure that the job description only has a one-year shelf life before it's reviewed. Having that once-a-year performance review is vital to keep a proper check on the size of your job.

Preparing for your new job description

Sometimes there are well-tested ideas, policies and working documents to take from your old school. These are probably more useful than trying to read new handbooks, policy statements and staff lists from your new school, or indeed diagrams about how to get round its new buildings. All of this is still names, faces and places that have no real human significance, whereas anything you've done well in the past needs to be preserved as it may be applicable in your new workplace, once you have got to know it properly.

The first week

When you step into your new school, you'll have to build up your reputation with staff and pupils from scratch. If you a new member of the SMT, a lot of people will expect you to slot into place very quickly. In a sense, you will be expected to hit the ground running and quickly establish a semblance of ownership of your line-management responsibilities.

The first absolute must is to sort out your office or workspace and get keys to classrooms and communal areas you need to use regularly. One of the best initial steps is preparing your lessons carefully to make a good first impression on the pupils you teach. Get in early and take an assembly in which the pupils and staff have a first taste of listening to you in a positive and entertaining forum. A good maiden assembly will get you off to a very good start, whereas losing a confrontation with a group of pupils larking around in the corridor and late for their lessons will not.

Look, listen and learn

In that first week and beyond, try and assimilate the customs and practices of your new school. Much of this first few days is about looking, listening and learning. These first conversations with staff are about hearing their ideas and having the existing systems explained to you. It's sensible to remain very non-committal at this point and go with the flow.

Being new will mean that you have a freshness and innocence of the ways in which business gets done and people interact. You won't understand the repetitive jealousies and rivalries, nor the constructive relationships of the school. In this situation your 'innocent' enthusiasms can make little tweaks to the systems, which staff can't resist because they know you haven't got immersed in the local politics and can't, as yet, have an axe to grind against anybody.

One case in point was a head of year I found myself line managing. In our first meeting she went through a catalogue of problems about school uniform, not just for her year group but across the whole school. Because I was blissfully unaware that her obsession with uniform was part of her wider critique of the inadequacies of the senior management team, I persuaded her to take a whole-school lead on uniform enforcement. She was taken by surprise by the prospect of getting a lead role and I was able to negotiate an extra management point for her. Almost by accident, I had stumbled on a solution to a problem that had been festering for years. There was no better person in this institution to enforce the uniform, but nobody had thought of offering her an opportunity to do this because they had been put off by the way she had used uniform problems to criticise senior management. Your 'newness' and naivety can lead you to ask the unthinkable question and broker the unlikely solution that has been sat in front of people's noses, but because of a history of antagonism can no longer be seen.

However, because of your initial naivety and innocence, some staff and pupils can use that lack of knowledge of local traditions and the existing status quo 'to try it on'. The obvious pupil action is to use the fact that you don't know who they are to defy you in a crowd-control situation in a corridor or lunch queue, maybe even to run away from the scene of the crime. Most staff around you will step in and help out but others will stand back and entertain themselves by watching your first public struggles to assert your authority. As we shall see in Chapter 7, no public confrontation is really lost if you follow up in the right way. In those first few days you need to do everything recommended in that chapter, however time consuming, to follow up.

Some staff will exploit your newness to school systems in other ways. When I was the school timetabler in my second senior post, I inherited a timetable that had been written the previous summer by somebody who had left the school. That did not stop the head of science coming to see me to get a room change. His request seemed perfectly logical as he wanted to swop a non-specialist room for a science lab. However, he failed to tell me that the lab had been given over to a technology class because in Year 8 technology there were less teachers and therefore much bigger classes than in science. Hence, technology needed the larger workspace – the science lab. Then there were the staff who asked me probing questions about what they should do about the implementation of this or that school policy. Obviously I didn't know the answer as yet, so when I stalled on an answer on the basis of my limited knowledge, they were quick to comment, 'But you're the deputy head!'

In the first week I regularly failed to answer questions, but often promised to get back to a person later. I made a really big effort to stick to this commitment, to begin to build a reputation for being reliable. Equally, in all my senior management jobs with a new headteacher, I tried to deliver a result quickly and effectively on something that I had been asked to do, even if it was only a small thing, to set up early signals that I was a safe pair of hands.

Part 2

Building the vital relationships

Chapter 4

Relationships with the teaching staff

In this chapter we look at:

- making good relationships with all of the staff;
- getting to know the personalities of staff and learning how to adjust for their strengths and weaknesses;
- the need to balance 'supervision' of what the staff do with 'support';
- managing by consensus and collaboration, rather than commanding;
- learning strategies for avoiding public confrontations and discussing sensitive issues behind closed doors;
- not letting your feelings of frustration with some individuals get the better of you: if you are accused of being a bully, your headteacher will probably be reluctant to support you;
- being realistic: schools are places in which endless compromises are the norm – it's often easier to bypass an awkward or inefficient individual and get somebody else to do it than get into a long running battle about it.

Setting the scene

You can only be an effective senior manager if you build good relationships with the staff. A lot of those new relationships are not as daily and direct as you will have been used to as a middle manager. They also involve 'collaborating' with others to get the job done, rather than commanding others to adhere to your master plan.

When you manage and lead people at your new more senior level, you are often listening to what they say they are doing with their own teams of staff. Line-management meetings with them become the opportunity to chart their progress in interactions with others. You work by orchestrating their work, for the most part letting them get on with something but occasionally prompting them to do it differently or steering them more insistently in a different direction. Managing the middle managers is like holding the snooker cue extension while another player takes the shot at the ball. The job requires a sophisticated blend of skills, the first being varying levels of supervision. You need to know when to hold onto leadership of an issue as the senior manager by structuring the steps of an intervention and when to let go completely and let all the initiative and judgement go to your colleague, simply keeping a watching eye on what they are doing.

But letting go of a process, through delegation, should never mean getting your middle managers to do all the work, while you sit back and listen to their exploits. It is necessary to intervene and support the other person, making sure that you use your senior position to open doors for them, so that their path to the goal is easier. I am going to describe this as 'servicing' the needs of the people you line manage.

Here are some examples of support and supervision that illustrate the balance between the two activities.

Case study I

I line managed the media resource officer in a school. She had been getting increasingly stressed because she had fallen behind on deadlines to produce a huge amount of photocopying and lamination for the English department. I listened carefully to her account of how she had fallen behind. 'Supporting' her as a senior manager didn't mean that I offered to do a two-hour stint of photocopying for her. (However, sometimes a gesture of support like this is not so far-fetched.) Rather, I could use my senior management role to get other people to support her in unblocking the problems. I got office staff drafted in for three mornings in a row to shift the backlog and help her catch up. I reminded staff, through our weekly bulletin, of the time factor on small, medium and large reprographic jobs. By doing this, I also reminded the media resource officer herself that she had deadlines which she was meant to be working to. Staff had been prompted by me to ask for 'due dates' from her and she agreed with me that she would stick to them. The little episode had reaffirmed her accountability to the staff, whilst reminding them that they couldn't overburden her.

I explored other ways of relieving her workload by asking the headteacher if we could cut the weekly newsletter down to a monthly one. He was unwilling, but the request prompted him to consider allocating the production of the newsletter to somebody else. The office receptionists agreed to take over the lamination machine and put things through it whenever they got a lull in their work. I tried to negotiate with the English department for them to do some of their own reprographics, using their own learning support assistant. It seemed like a good idea, but I didn't get anywhere with that one as there were some deep-seated personnel/job description issues, which were being dealt with directly by the headteacher.

All of these manoeuvres behind the scenes helped unblock a problem and tighten systems, as well as ease my colleague's difficulties with her job. Some worked as a short-term measure and some re-established systems that had been temporarily forgotten. One approach fell flat on its face. As a senior manager, you have to get used to being patient and grateful for getting a partial result on what you set out to achieve.

Case study 2

The second case study centres on a major curriculum initiative around teaching. All schools are obsessed with raising their exam results and it is common for senior managers to bear down on heads of department with the 'what are you going to do about it?' routine.

As a senior manager responsible for student data, I had become increasingly conscious that we had bombarded our departments with so much data about our pupils that they were completely confused by it all. Line-management feedback to me made it quite clear that I needed to re-launch the student data in a much more accessible way. If the departments were going to use data analysis to improve results, then I had to 'support' them as a senior manager by 'servicing their needs' – by thinking of a more meaningful way of giving them the data.

The 'meaningful' came quickly to mean 'eye catching' and entertaining. I rearranged the Year 11 into a league table with pupils on the highest combined SATs scores at the top of it. The premier division of combined SATs scores of at least 17 points (e.g. science – level 5, maths – 6 and English – 6) invariably got their five A to C grades. But pupils with combined point scores of 15 or more, according to my analysis that compared SATs results with GCSE outcomes, had a 60 per cent probability of converting to five A to C grades. At a lower points score than this, their only chance of gaining five A to C grades equivalence was to pass the GNVQ ICT, worth up to four GCSEs in one go. The rank-order league table created a group of twenty-five borderline candidates. To draw attention to them, I labelled them our 'key marginals' – the seats we had to win if we were to secure election victory. Focusing on such a small number of our Year 11s really helped the heads of subject mount a proper intervention programme for them. They now responded to the league table with more focus and enthusiasm.

I was able to service their needs further by drawing upon my team of learning support teachers and assistants to go into class and help get late coursework finished properly. We were able to pick off 'key marginals' in subjects where they were closest to obtaining grade Cs. Most importantly, I was able to divert our most computer literate learning support assistant to the GNVQ ICT on a semi-permanent basis. This was the key area where Year 11s could pick up four A to C grades in one go, leaving just one C outstanding from another curriculum area. Sometimes the 'servicing role' of the senior manager is to galvanise a school improvement process and bring all the most important ingredients, from each part of the school, together and integrate them. It will be a senior manager such as you who will see where to unblock a problem and divert resources from one place to another.

For the first time in a long time, I had been able to produce data on students and advertise it to staff in a way that actually held their interest. Having captured the audience, I had been able to provide them with extra staffing resources, which had empowered them to work more effectively with a small group of Year 11 pupils. To be a good senior manager, 'getting alongside' the people and the things they have to do is vital. You have to help them make things happen, not just tell them what to do. In the case study of the student data, I often serviced the staff in a very basic way. Teachers have a habit of losing data you give them. They are so busy that they often misplace paper or forget how to download it from the computer. Even though I have given them the information before,

I did it again and again, if necessary. As their line manager, I wanted to nurture and preserve any spark of interest they were showing about the initiative I was leading.

Following the personal narratives

Much of your day, as a deputy headteacher, is spent following an account of what other middle managers are doing directly with their teams. The narrative you listen to, and occasionally attempt to shape, can be distorted in a number of unhelpful and unproductive ways. When you start to build relationships with the staff, you begin to learn the pitfalls of following their personal narratives. To learn how to interpret personal narratives, you have to become proficient at conducting different types of 'reality checks', based on your knowledge of their individual personalities.

The positive spin reality check

Some middle managers have a way of spinning it like it's all happening perfectly. I used to meet a head of year who made me feel very content. Any question I asked her about the work she was doing, she appeared to have got it covered and more. She never brought me problems unless she was also ready to suggest possible solutions. She was a dream to work with and yet the substance of her work behind that glowing facade was superficial. I grew to appreciate that I had to check up on what she said she had done. I also came to learn that I had to take more of the driver's seat on work she was handling, even though she seemed so comfortable about being proactive about any task.

As a deputy headteacher or assistant headteacher you must learn to be on your guard against the positive spin of some of those you line manage. Positive spinning is a persistent disease in our modern society, especially in education, and is one of the main causes why problems are not analysed honestly and effective solutions found.

The negative spin reality check

For every 'it's all going well and I'm on top of it' merchant, there is the negative spinner. They moan and complain about everything they are asked to do, yet often go away and work through it all effectively and efficiently. They are happy to tell you that what you request of them is a waste of time and then go away and execute it better than you could have done yourself. They ignore your advice or instructions pointedly when in a line-management meeting with you, only to take it a few days or weeks later. In many ways, they are a more reliable breed of manager to work with than the positive spinners.

The 'you are bullying me' reality check

A few people who disagree with you about everything you want to do and have an endless series of arguments about why they shouldn't do it can be very dangerous to you. Unlike the negative spinners, who moan but ultimately co-operate efficiently, this smaller group of individuals take a very different approach to being managed and led.

I have dealt occasionally with a few individuals who will argue and disagree with you about everything you want them to consider doing. Even when you patiently negotiate a compromise solution, they won't embrace it truly. If you try and force the issue, however gently, they accuse you of trying to bully them. By this stage in the proceeding this interpretation is probably party true and I know I have clearly shown my frustration and exasperation at their non-cooperation to such an extent, that at the very least I have spoken somewhat sharply to them.

Being accused of 'bullying' is a very bad result for you, whether totally just or not. We shall see later in this chapter that head-teachers will not always back you up, even though they may have asked you to be a 'tough manager'.

The floaters reality check

But not all forms of non-cooperation are belligerent. Some teachers whom you line manage just cannot do what you want them to. The flesh is willing but the skills of going about organising the school aspect of their lives are simply not there. The floaters fail all forms of reality check on their work. One example is a colleague I line managed and who was utterly supportive and willing to please. But he just couldn't organise himself beyond the present moment. Whatever encouragement or help I gave him, he could only stick to that purpose for one or two days before the need to return and finish off the job properly just floated away from his mind. Trying to change him was impossible and one simply had to go with his flow and work in the 'here and now', tapping into his goodwill and wish to co-operate.

Piggy in the middle

As a deputy or assistant headteacher you are often caught between the headteacher and the rest of the staff, both sides wanting you to see the issue from their point of view and sometimes hoping you will present their point of view to the other side. Heads of department and teachers will often line you up and sound you out, feeling more comfortable with telling you about something that they would not go to the headteacher about. They want you to take their opinion to the headteacher, maybe trusting that you will find a diplomatic way of expressing their view. Headteachers themselves rely on this type of 'grapevine' information from their senior managers to help them gauge public opinion. They also rely on their senior managers taking their leadership message and playing it to the members of staff in a way that will encourage them to incorporate it.

Being buttonholed and bombarded everywhere you go

As a deputy headteacher I sometimes find it difficult to move from point A to B in the school without being 'buttonholed' by pupils, parents, teachers or office staff. We will look at how to handle the constant stress of people trying to cut a slice off you, wherever you are going and whatever the separate agenda you are trying to pursue. In challenging, inner-city schools this problem is more prevalent. You only need to walk down one of your corridors to find a teacher who needs help with an aggressive pupil or a truant who must be taken to a lesson. A teacher will pounce on you, seeking clarification on some school organisational point or have a long moan about one. In some ways, it is a good sign that people want to bombard you with their questions and problems. The fact that they see you as a sponge, shock absorber or fount of information means that you have established meaningful relationships within the school. But you must balance the necessity to 'support and service' the needs of the staff with your own imperatives to fulfil other aspects of your job description, without becoming unbearably stressed.

Monkey on the shoulder

My current headteacher taught me a good technique for avoiding getting completely overwhelmed with ownership of teachers' problems. When somebody has explained their difficulty to you, don't automatically take the 'monkey' off them and put it on your own shoulder. Instead, suggest ways forward with the problem that they may not have thought of themselves, ways that leave the next step with them. Have you seen X or have you involved your line manager Y? What about meeting Z and testing out her opinion? That way, the monkey stays on the shoulder of the person who brings it, instead of a lot of monkeys gathering all over you, until you collapse under their weight.

Remembering this technique is vital. You need to support and service the staff you manage, but that cannot mean taking over all their problems. Your advice, after reflecting on their difficulties, must sometimes be all that you can offer.

Strategies for handling the difficult staffing situations

You will handle difficult characters on the staff most effectively when you first learn how to handle yourself. All senior managers need to monitor their own behaviour as soon as they find themselves involved in a difficult situation. The first step to doing that effectively is to recognise when you've arrived in one.

When somebody comes at you, ready to give you a verbal pasting about something which they are unhappy about and want to blame you or the SMT in general, try and get out of the public place. If it's happening in the staff room, with a large audience, it is more likely that you and the teacher making the scene will explode into full-scale argument, because of the feeling that you are about to lose face in front of others. The tendency to play to the gallery can feel overwhelming for both parties!

Those difficult conversations about your role and somebody else's part in a complex piece of organisation have to be discussed with honesty. That discussion must be done in private if it is to have any real chance of producing a positive result. You should consider the following points:

- Walk away from that aggressive member of staff rather than get angry yourself and get sucked into a confrontation.
- When you have got them on their own behind a closed door, give them a proper chance to have their say.
- Look for any positives in the work of the person you are managing. Frame any critical comments you have around those positive comments.
- Try and stay as relaxed as possible about the interchange, however annoyed you feel inside.
- Be prepared, if you have to, to grit your teeth and confront the other person with what you believe the key problem is.
- Look for a constructive way forward from a difficult situation. It's likely to be some form of compromise on what you would have ideally wanted, but it should provide an element of 'win–win' to both sides.

In the most extreme situation I have encountered, I told a member of staff I would not talk to them unless they stopped shouting. I warned them I would walk away and when the tirade persisted, I did walk away. The teacher followed me down the stairs, out of the school and up the road. By that time neither of us were talking and the comedy of the situation suddenly dawned on both of us. The tension dispelled and the constructive conversation could take place.

A more frequent occurrence is being stopped by a member of staff in a corridor to be moaned at about something. A small queue then develops as others line up to bring their worries and concerns. In a situation like this, you can find yourself taking the communal blame for the sins of the whole SMT over all aspects of school organisation. It is important to concentrate on staying relaxed. The more someone has got you as 'piggy in the middle' in a dispute, the more you must consciously choose to sidestep confrontation in that public space. And sometimes it pays to disarm the onslaught of your attacker by admitting you have made a mistake and apologising for it. Even if a problem is by no means all your fault, saying sorry for the part of it that might be your fault is always a sensible way of taking the wind out of the sails of the complainant. Learning to be the first one to say sorry is a vital senior management skill.

In watching yourself and how you behave, it helps to monitor your own behaviour for dangerous lapses of sexism or even unconscious racism. Are you letting some negative stereotypes creep into the way you are handling the situation with some people?

I often try and picture myself, sitting on my hands, if the interchange is getting tetchy. In the past, I have not always been able to keep this up and my exasperation has finally got the better of me. I have snapped back at the other person! If you do this, you open yourself to the eventual charge that you are trying to bully and intimidate.

Support from headteachers with difficult staff

I have found that headteachers often talk about managing staff 'tough' but that in reality they will seldom support you if you pursue a member of staff too vigorously. In the end, the middle managers who are squeezed for every inch of productivity are the very conscientious, hard-working ones. More and more is put onto them, while a minority of inefficient or obstructive staff are gone round and simply left alone.

If you persuade a difficult member of staff to do more than they usually would, then the headteacher will be pleased. If you fail and get accused of being a bully, the only safe course of action is to back off immediately and apologise (whether you have done anything wrong or not). Ultimately, you must manage people with a series of compromises around what you want from them and what they are choosing to give. Busy schools are such demanding places that it simply doesn't make sense to turn the screw too tightly on other colleagues.

I have learned my lesson from several difficult situations over the years. Invariably, I have made matters worse by being too persistent in challenging other people. If they are not going to respond to my initial advice and suggestions on how to do something, they are only likely to become more difficult and stubborn if I persist in trying to get them to do what I want. Perhaps a headteacher has more weapons at their disposal, but as a senior manager you need to take a more circuitous route.

Handling conflict between staff

A senior team member often has to mediate on disputes between colleagues. When I'm faced with one of these situations I always begin by taking stock and listening carefully to each person's account of what has gone wrong. In the first instance I would show that I empathised with how the complainant was feeling. Then try and point out to them what the issues and feelings of the other persons involved might be. Sometimes, it is enough to make it clear that there is not a conspiracy but simply a 'cock up' in the school's organisation that has led to the problem. Often a conversation like this is enough for both adversaries to get together themselves and sort their way through a problem. On other occasions, I have had to bring people together and mediate, insisting that they give each other the time and space to listen to each other's point of view. However, mediation is not always possible, especially if there is a long history of bitterness and antagonism between two teachers. Getting them together is likely to open a 'can of worms' rather than resolve the present issue. In these circumstances, the trusted senior school manager's tool is brought into play: go round the problem and get the job done in some other way, using different personnel. Taking the least point of resistance is a common habit when running a busy, complex school. Frequently, pragmatism rather than justice or equality for the staff is the guiding principle behind the way senior managers sort out an immediate organisational problem in their school.

Case study 1

Here's a typical example of a situation where you might be called upon to mediate.

Ruth was a learning support assistant attached to the humanities department and working with special needs statemented pupils in their lessons. She came to me to complain about the new humanities teacher, who she said had both a racist and sexist attitude towards her and a racist attitude towards the history he was teaching the pupils. I went through what had been done and said. It was clear that Ruth was not being given the opportunity to take as active a role in the lesson as she had become accustomed to. She was a highly intelligent Afro-Caribbean, a single mother who was well on the way to getting a degree and would likely as not be a history teacher herself within a couple of years. Mr Tyson was a young, newly qualified teacher who was very anxious to prove he could control his classes. I asked Ruth to speak to Mr Tyson on her own in the first instance, explaining to him just how she was feeling. I suggested to her that she might point out her personal response to some of his points about the British Empire. Apparently, the conversation had taken place but Ruth came straight back to me saying that Mr Tyson had demonstrated all his traits of racism and chauvinism and dismissed her out of hand. I said that I would speak to Mr Tyson and found that he was indeed very defensive about the contents of his lessons being challenged in any way by a learning support assistant. However, his description of his teaching on imperialism came over as thoughtful and sensible to me.

I decided to get them together with me for an active mediation. With a third person present, neither party wanted to look unreasonable and they curbed the worst of their excesses and gave each other a real chance to explain their positions. It soon became obvious that the differences between them were much less than had been mutually anticipated. Indeed, they seemed to see eye to eye on many things. Perhaps for the very first time, Mr Tyson began to see Ruth as an intelligent asset in his room.

What I learnt

Complex human interactions that have gone wrong need both time and attention to detail to sort out. If you can get people to listen to each other properly, then you've got a good chance of resolving the problems well. This situation unravelled itself positively but many other school impasses do not. The very sticky ones are usually bypassed by school senior managers in their habitual quest to find the least point of resistance in getting what they want completed.

Case study 2

The second example of how to broker a solution on a typical kind of dispute between staff concerns a bust-up between the head of special needs and the exams officer. The argument was about the end of Key Stage Three exams for 14-year-olds, currently called the SATs. The exams officer wanted the main exam hall to be free of all possible behaviourally challenging pupils. The head of special needs had agreed a definite list of pupils to be withdrawn to do the exam with the learning support department. They were a motley crew of challenging hard cases! Nevertheless, at the last moment the exams officer sent off one more difficult pupil, not on the list, as well as a girl who was having a panic attack and refused to sit her paper in the big hall. The two members of staff had a big public bust-up in front of pupils and teachers, with the head of special needs accepting the extras very grudgingly.

As in the first case study, the key is to follow up with a conversation with both these managers separately, to get an idea of what happened and why. The head of special needs must understand that the exams officer had no choice but to offload the semi-hysterical exam refuser. There was no opportunity to have a long public debate with her. On the other hand, sending an additional behaviourally challenging child to the learning support department, when they had their hands full was just not fair. Both are just about able to accept each other's viewpoints without my being there to mediate. I am able to support their rapprochement in my role as senior manager by proposing that an additional learning mentor be there for the rest of the exam cycle to take any last-minute problem pupils to another location to do the exam. Once again, a strategic overview of all the resources in the school has given me a chance to find an alternative answer to a niggling problem. Because I line managed the learning mentors as well as special needs and exams, this was a very easy solution to come up with. There will be occasions when you will need to liaise with the headteacher and the rest of the SMT to come up with a sensible solution to school-wide problems.

Key strategies for handling conflict between staff effectively

1 Provide opportunities for everyone involved in the conflict to talk to you separately. Set aside at least half an hour so you can listen in an unhurried way.
2 Draw them out by leading them into saying how they feel. Get rid of the desk if you usually sit behind one and draw chairs closer. (The 90 degree angle is far less threatening.)
3 Offer them a hot drink.
4 If you are going to get somebody to confide in you, they will need a lot of reassuring and you might well be seen as

threatening because of your senior position. Getting over this takes a lot of listening and very little talking, except to ask the occasional open-ended clarification like 'How did that make you feel?' Some eye contact and regular summarising of what you think somebody has said to you help.

5 Explore a number of possible solutions to their problem, but essentially try to get the person themself to arrive at their own conclusion, with a bit of prompting from you.
6 Towards the end of the process, it is likely that you'll have to break with the role of counsellor and view the issue in terms of the management of the school. But if the member of staff you've been counselling has had a chance to talk something through, they are more likely to accept your change of remit.

Overall conclusion on leading and managing staff

The key to success in any senior management position is to try and stay relaxed in the face of high levels of friction, annoyance and calamity. For me, that means fitting in with a boxing analogy and staying light on my feet in the ring. If I dance around my problems like Muhammad Ali, jabbing at my opponents as they come for me and then moving away, I usually do quite well. At least a draw on points! When I get heavy-footed and decide to stand and trade punches on the ropes with a problem, I always end up making a mess of it. Being heavy-handed as a senior manager in a complex, stressful place like school is a recipe for confrontation and lots of aggravation. There's enough friction with the pupils, let alone falling out with the staff as well.

Vital in your campaign to stay relaxed is not to take any of it too seriously, particularly the endless initiatives of the government's school improvement agenda. If you stay relaxed and see the humourous, indeed ridiculous, side of all this frantic displacement activity from the bureaucracy, you will gain the respect of the staff you work with as a person of integrity. This doesn't mean to say you are cynical, but that you remain loyal to your own educational vision and prioritise only what is useful and practical for your school from a myriad of government policies.

Finally, you need to watch your own body language, not only when you are interacting with staff but when you are moving around the building, as members of staff can be watching you at any time. Like any human being, senior managers have days when they are tired, flat, frustrated or disconsolate in some way. Try not to let it show. People are expecting you to be positive and upbeat, even when you are not feeling it. I mention this because it's something I really have to watch in myself on dark, cold, wintery mornings or when I've been brought a grizzly emergency to deal with by one of my colleagues, just as I was settling down to do some of my own paper work. We will look at how to preserve yourself in a tough multi-tasking environment in Chapter 11.

Chapter 5

Building a relationship with your headteacher

In this chapter we look at:

- the vast array of personal styles that people approach headship with;
- keeping an effective relationship with your boss: without it, your power to influence the school will be seriously limited;
- tactical moves that will help you keep in with the headteacher;
- what will be happening if the relationship between headteacher and the senior manager is good.

I have worked with five different headteachers in three schools as a senior manager and another four as a head of department. Over the years I talked to countless deputy headteachers about the vast variety of leadership styles on offer from headteachers. The only constant feature of headship is that because of the varied personalities of those who take on the role, they each do it very differently. As a member of the senior management team, you are going to have to find a way of adapting to what you've got. If that person has appointed you in the first place, then at least you have got initial goodwill on your side.

My examples of headteacher archetypes will give you a flavour of some of varieties of temperament to expect. I have never worked for a headteacher who didn't have good and bad points. Some had weaknesses that are my strengths, but many were good at things that I always struggle with.

The emotionally volatile headteacher

If you have trouble controlling your emotions, headship is the kind of job to really bring that out. One headteacher I worked with was either 'sunny' or 'sulky' and seemed to have a very thin skin. He would walk around on some days with a cloud over his head and his deputy headteachers became very wary of his moods. Despite this, he was very hard working and committed to his educational vision for the school. This aspect of his personality led the staff to give him a grudging respect. They were in no doubt about the things that he valued.

The intellectually challenging headteacher

Another headteacher I worked with conformed to a different regular pattern. He sounded utterly inspirational in a meeting with fellow educationalists talking about his vision. But he was far less effective at making it happen in the reality of a large secondary school and failed to convince a large section of the teaching staff that what he wanted to do was right. He also failed to set up efficient systems for managing the daily running of the school and so, ultimately, the intellectually challenging lead came to nothing.

The commanding headteacher

Another typical model of headship is the cut-and-thrust 'take no prisoners' headteacher. I've worked for one of these as well and she seemed to positively relish dominating those around her. The school had an energetic feel to it but there was no real thought or proper evaluation about how to improve the education on offer. The level of debate on improvement was rushed, but the day-to-day systems were strong.

These three examples demonstrate a simple point: a school becomes the reflection of its leader's strengths and weaknesses. As a member of that person's SMT, you need to find out as quickly as you can what those are and find a way of slotting yourself in alongside them. Nowadays, few headteachers are truly radical on educational issues. The pressure put on them by central government and local education authorities to follow prescribed school improvement initiatives and the National Curriculum pressurise them into conformity and discourage risk-taking. The typical twenty-first-century headteacher has to appease so many educational stakeholders, performing a complex balancing act with pupils, parents, governors, inspectors, local authority advisers, politicians, social services and the local and national media. Given that the individuals who make it to headship are personally ambitious, their number one agenda often ends up being the same as that of a hard-bitten politician – self-preservation and self-promotion. Headteachers do what they need to do to hold onto power and advance themselves. This doesn't mean that they can't or won't be supportive to their senior managers or don't genuinely wish to improve the fortunes of the pupils in their schools. But ultimately, most headteachers, whatever their good or bad points, want to be seen as personally effective and successful. You must always be slightly wary of doing anything that could jeopardise this success for them and if they see you as a barrier to their 'glowing reputation', many will be utterly ruthless in attacking or marginalising you. As one colleague once explained to me, in a really difficult situation where tough decisions had to be taken, the headteacher moved away from the rest of the staff and set up a distance from which to wield the sword. Saving herself and her own reputation had become the key objective.

How well your relationship works with your headteacher depends on your personal chemistry with them. In one school, you could be pressed into acting like the headteacher's personal assistant and in another school have a huge amount of autonomy and a chance to use your initiative. With some headteachers you will feel like a dogsbody, with others, your relationship will flower into a brilliant partnership.

How to manage your headteacher

Fortune will deal you its own hand of cards. The interview process should usually give you an indication of what a potential headteacher is like and if you don't feel comfortable with the personality and leadership style you are witnessing, don't take the job at the school.

Once you are in post, you will have to work very hard at keeping the relationship with the headteacher constructive. Without that, you cannot have any power or influence in the school as one of the senior managers. Most headteachers will try and be as reasonable as they can with a new deputy headteacher as they need a productive relationship with you as much as you need it with them. If you're lucky, they will have been deputy headteachers recently enough themselves to remember the inherent tensions and difficulties of the job. But if there are problems, it's a bigger challenge for you to 'manage up' the hierarchy to make the relationship with your boss work than the other way round. If the relationship with your headteacher becomes difficult, persevering to improve it is an excellent learning experience for managing almost any difficult staffing situation you will be faced with, as either deputy or headteacher in future years.

Practical tips to maintain a good relationship with the headteacher

- Meet your deadlines.
- When you write up a report or action plan, think it through properly so you are ready for any critique that could come from the headteacher. As in all school situations, be ready to compromise on your original plan, without taking personal offence.
- Don't be seen as a person who is trying to upstage the headteacher.
- Once the headteacher has discovered your weaknesses, take responsibility for them and show willingness to work on them. Everybody has things they don't like doing or find difficult to do well. What your boss will be looking for from you is a self-awareness on those wobbly areas, a willingness to admit to a mistake and do better next time.
- When you disagree with the headteacher, do it in private and not in public. In the context of a big secondary school this means in a one-to-one line-management meeting and not in the senior management team itself.
- In situations where the headteacher has got a clear consensus from the rest of the SMT on an issue with which you disagree, try and stay quiet about it in public. Sticking to collegial loyalty is important for the unity and effectiveness of the overall leadership of the school. The staff need to see the headteacher and SMT working harmoniously.
- Save your energy for arguments on 'big things' and support your headteacher on all the little ones.

The characteristics of a good partnership

You will know you have a good partnership with your current headteacher when you can answer most of the following statements with a 'yes'. Underpinning any effective working relationship is good two-way communication, based on trust.

1. You understand how to get the best out of your headteacher and vice versa. This means both sides understand each other's strengths and weaknesses.
2. You stick up for your headteacher in their absence and when working with third parties. The same applies the other way round.
3. You feel comfortable to explore issues with the headteacher honestly, rather than telling them what they want to hear.
4. You can give the headteacher reliable advice on what the staff are thinking and how they would react to particular initiatives.
5. You meet regularly and talk fully about the management issues that concern the school.
6. In these meetings, you are totally confident that you can come up with ideas and initiatives yourself and that they will be appreciated.
7. You feel comfortable asking for advice and guidance from your headteacher when you are unsure what to do about something.

Chapter 6

Relationships in the senior management team

In this chapter we look at:

- what it looks like when you've got a very good senior management team;
- the key characteristics of a team that is not functioning well;
- the regular pitfalls of senior management meetings;
- dealing with conflict between yourself and other members of the SMT.

Questions to ask about the SMT you are joining

You should ask these questions and know the answers to them within a term of joining your new management team.

- How have the other team members evolved into their current positions? Are they internal appointments? Were they external appointments? Did the current headteacher appoint them?
- What is the history of relationships within this team?
- Who is 'highly regarded' by the headteacher? In what circumstances does the headteacher listen to them?
- Who, if anyone, is marginalised?
- How well are SMT meetings structured and the business of the school handled?
- Is this SMT a rubber stamp for the headteacher or is there real discussion?

- Does this SMT moan about the rest of the staff and blame them for problems in the school?

The role of SMT

The senior management team assists the headteacher in the running of the school. The headteacher takes overall responsibility for this job but delegates parts of it to the deputy and assistant headteachers because the work is so wide-ranging, varied and complicated.

At one level, running things means making sure that the school operates day to day, but 'running things' also implies that as a member of the SMT you are a part of an advisory group for the creation and implementation of school policy. As we have already seen, as a senior manager, you now become a team member rather than the direct team leader of a year group or department. You may well be joining a long-established team of managers, who have worked together under the same headteacher for many years. This could put a lot of pressure on you to conform to the ways of the group. Conversely, your headteacher may have appointed you to shake things up and challenge the way business is conducted. Sometimes you could find yourself a part of a newly formed team and in a situation where the balance of relationships is going to be freshly worked out. One piece of management jargon which vividly sums up the process that goes on when a new group of individuals have to come together for the first time or a significant new individual has been added to an established group is that 'storming and norming' will take place. The 'storming' stage is when sparks fly as the group jostles for position and influence in the new team. Most personality clashes take place at this stage. Once people have got used to each other's styles and viewpoints, a period of 'norming' takes place and the team settles down, with members evolving into roles that largely mirror their individual strengths and weaknesses.

Overlapping job descriptions

As a senior team member, much of your job description will be your own but roles can overlap, especially ones like maintaining pupil discipline across the school or dealing with emergencies. A large strategic remit like exams will often have two or more senior managers making significant inputs. One deputy headteacher may be dealing with the technical issues of getting the right exam papers on the desks and another senior manager overseeing the behaviour of the pupils as they go in and out of the exam room. In these overlapping jurisdictions, people have to agree about how to share power and, as we shall see, this can be a source of tension and misunderstanding.

Conflicting job descriptions

Some aspects of assistant/deputy headteacher job descriptions do not merely overlap, they contradict each other. For example, one deputy headteacher has responsibility for putting an enrichment programme together for able and gifted students and another deputy has a remit for running peer mentoring in which some students help younger pupils learn to read better. A third assistant headteacher is responsible for daily events in the school like running fire drill, arranging the BCG injections or the visit of the school photographer. Unless there is very close liaison at SMT level, all three of these senior managers' duties could clash. The deputy who pushes for a thorough enrichment programme could be taking the wind out of the sails of their colleague who wants to use able pupils to help with the reading. The enrichment classes could be getting in the way of a planned visit from the school photographer. In such situations, tension between senior team members is possible as each person is in direct competition, wanting the headteacher to see them as successful in fulfilling their individual job description.

Likewise, other conflicts of interest can occur for a new senior manager. In your last job, you were the head of science and now you have a strategic whole-school management remit for teaching and learning, you must guard against giving your old subject a bigger share of the resources than anybody else, just because you are familiar with the needs of a science department.

Good leadership of SMT

What you can be sure of is that there will be jealousies and rivalries lurking below the surface in the SMT. They will be best contained by a headteacher who is a good team manager and is acutely aware of people's strengths and weaknesses and how to incorporate them positively. Some headteachers I have worked with have not been able to, or have not wished to, resolve these de-stabilising rivalries.

An efficient SMT will be a major driving force for good in the school. It will help unblock problems and keep the school running smoothly and it will be a place in which new developments can be carefully planned, implemented and evaluated. A bad SMT can be completely dysfunctional, adding to the problems of communication in a school and ultimately disempowering the middle managers and ordinary teachers.

Features of an efficient SMT

- All members are capable of forming a whole-school view. They can contribute and lead on policy-making and implementation.
- They get the right personal balance between leadership on the 'big things' and management of the small practical details.
- Members of the team are self-confident and adaptable enough to share responsibilities with each other.
- Team members are capable of multi-tasking within their own job descriptions, whilst still contributing to the work of the whole team.
- Although they report directly to the headteacher, they have a strong daily working relationship with each other.
- Members of the team have an awareness of each other's talents and can compensate for each other's weaknesses.

The features of a dysfunctional SMT

- Too many team members spend too much time on administration and paper work.
- This leads them to stay in their office too much, concentrating on running routine systems that could be delegated to non-teaching staff.
- They don't have the strategic whole-school view and are not leading on school curriculum development.
- Members of the team show no interest in probing the issues of teaching and learning in the school and are often in 'auto pilot' with their own classroom teaching.
- Members of the team are reactive and not pro-active. Middle managers don't spend time with them and instead go straight to the headteacher.
- Team members are short on leadership skills but are unaware or unwilling to admit to it. Thus they are missing the key senior

management skills – those of self-reflection and honest self-criticism.

Senior management meetings – the reality

Most schools have SMTs that work at a level somewhere between the scenarios described above. I've worked in SMTs where generally speaking most of the positive criteria are on show. But senior management meeting times often have shortcomings that stop them from functioning at their best. Before you enter one, you need to know what the limitations can be.

Sham discussion

Some headteachers do not bother to foster a team spirit and have often discussed issues with each deputy headteacher in a separate one-to-one line-management situation. So when the team meets, there is only limited discussion about the major issues as the truly significant talks have already happened elsewhere.

Then there are senior management meetings where there is a hollow pretence of discussion because the headteacher already has a position on the major issues and other individuals know that anything they say will not alter this. Some teams are discouraged from taking up discussion because they believe the headteacher has a favourite, whose opinion is always listened to above everybody else. Discussion can also be limited because the headteacher's usual way of seeking advice is to go directly to middle managers, leaving the senior team to form a rather pointless talking shop.

Ineffective discussion

Even when the senior team and headteacher work positively together, there is a tendency for complex daily organisation and management issues in a school to crowd out the vital probing educational discussions that are often needed to really take the school forward. I've noticed that there is a tendency to advocate the same old tired solutions to persistent problems. For example, a deputy headteacher reports that teachers are complaining about not getting support with difficult pupil behaviour. This has been a regular complaint in all the schools I have worked in, but it often generates a similar superficial response from senior management.

Perhaps some of the leadership team feel that the criticism is personally levelled at them because of their job description. Frequently they react to this complaint by blaming groups of staff outside senior management for failing to implement some aspect of school policy. So student behaviour is deemed to be poor because form tutors and heads of department are not doing their jobs properly. The management jargon for blaming others outside the direct team is called 'outgroup sourcing' and SMTs can spend a lot of time doing it. It is an understandable reaction in human terms. The senior management team has worked hard to have good relationships with each other and the headteacher, and nobody wants to risk being seen to blame one of their own number directly or indirectly. To preserve the group identity of the regular team, members of that team prefer to sling mud at others outside of the intimate group.

But the best teams seek to operate a 'no blame and shame' policy when discussing critical issues. They are aware of the danger of blaming others for their own failings as a team to lead the school. They are not afraid to think outside conventional lines and probe deeply into why something isn't working rather than 'outgroup source' it onto the rest of the staff. Such teams have individuals who don't spend their whole time trying to guess what is in the mind of their headteacher and echoing it back to them in the meeting.

Decisions that fall between stools and get lost

Many decisions taken in the SMT are not returned to at a later date because they get forgotten about. Nobody is sure what their exact role in the implementation of the plan is or when the subject will be returned to. All senior teams try and create a timescale and chain of responsibility during their meetings, but none that I have worked on have found a truly effective way of doing it. This is because at any single SMT meeting there are too many issues to discuss and plans of action to work out. Agendas become crowded with the highly complex business of just running the school, let alone talking about plans to improve it. Last-minute items find themselves on the discussion list under 'Any other Business' and there are simply too many topics to consider properly.

In the perfect school, the SMT would find a more effective way of organising and prioritising agendas, so that important issues get proper discussion and decision-making time. As it is, I have often been left confused as to which of us is supposed to be doing what and by when. Or indeed, if anyone is going to do anything at all. Some schools get round these problems by having occasional meetings where there is only one item on the agenda and ample time for a full discussion. Other school SMTs meet each morning to work out as much of the daily school organisation as possible, leaving more time for the bigger issue discussions in timetabled or after-school meeting time. Basically, the reality of senior management in busy schools is that there is always too much to do and too much to talk about. Once you start discussing a major educational issue, it always becomes more complicated than you had thought, producing side issues that could have never have been anticipated. It is something you must be prepared to accept when you enter a school leadership team.

Dealing with confrontation in the SMT

In Chapter 5 we advised that big clashes with the headteacher should be kept for one-to-one line-management meetings. If at all possible, confrontation with other SMT members are best dealt with in private. Firstly, they are more likely to be resolved through mutual compromise if they are not witnessed by large numbers of the staff. Once an audience has seen a disagreement, the personal pride at stake for both sides is always greater. Secondly, the headteacher will have a lower opinion of both protagonists if they are seen to squabble in public. Whenever possible, 'dirty linen' should be washed behind closed doors and the headteacher and other SMT members never need know about it.

However, in my experience, there are times when you must ask the headteacher to mediate in your relationship with another member of the SMT. On some occasions a quick word with both colleagues separately would be enough. In more serious disputes, getting both people together is the only way to nip serious problems in the bud.

In my time as a senior manager in three different schools, the major source of tension I have had to deal with is 'being put upon' by other members of the team. In the first type of situation, other members of the SMT have tried to delegate ('offload') parts of their work to me and I've had to protest. In the second type of situation, the headteacher has tried to give me the work of another member of the SMT, who hasn't been doing it effectively. In both situations I've had to fight to maintain the line between what my personal job description says and my general overlapping SMT responsibilities, which can place almost anything at my door. Having a dispute with another senior manager is always very difficult to deal with as you are in such close working proximity with each other all the time. Yet it is vital to the cohesion of the school and for your own peace of mind that the team is seen to be working together well and personal differences are ironed out before they start to fester.

Chapter 7

Relationships with the pupils and their parents

In this chapter we look at:

- issues around physical restraint for senior managers on corridor duty and crowd control situations in general;
- how to give pupils an effective telling off;
- how to carry out detective work in the student population, using hard cop, soft cop buddy relationships;
- being successful on senior management emergency rota and dealing with difficult pupils who refuse to leave the classroom;
- handling challenging parents.

Many senior managers will quickly become specialists at their job description in terms of analysing data, running exams, setting up cover or implementing a whole-school numeracy policy, but all will need to be at least 'competent' in handling pupils and their parents.

Building relationships with the pupils

An effective assistant/deputy headteacher will be able to create good relationships with pupils in and out of the classroom. This means being able to establish a 'presence' when pupils are misbehaving in other teachers' classrooms and in corridor situations. Being effective does not necessarily mean you have to become the most charismatic disciplinarian in the school or a regimental sergeant major, but it means that you can be called up to sort out difficult breakdowns in behaviour around the building and you can do so competently and confidently.

Being a good teacher

In Chapter 3, when discussing settling in to a SMT post, I advised you to make it a priority to teach your lessons well as a first base for being accepted in the school in a senior role. Good lessons begin the process of establishing trusting relationships with a group of pupils. Even if you only teach one hundred out of one thousand pupils, the message that your lessons are OK will spread out to the population as a positive signal. You put your first anchor down as senior manager by showing you are an effective teacher.

Doing good assemblies

After teaching some good lessons, it's useful to show yourself to the large part of student population in a positive light by giving some good assemblies. An entertaining and colourful message in this arena will set you up well for being seen as a figure of intellectual and moral authority around the school. If you do particularly well, pupils might question you further about the messages of your assemblies in the corridor. A good reputation will hold you in good stead in difficult situations where you are intervening with pupils you don't know but who will already know you.

In Chapter 10 we will look at the key skills a successful senior manager needs and will be examining how to make a presentation to large groups of teachers. The same principles apply to giving thought-provoking assemblies. Obviously, you can't make every assembly a theatrical masterpiece and the frequency with which you are expected to lead them will have an impact on your creativity. It's worth collecting good stories from newspapers at times when you are not on the rota and jotting down some ideas. The basis of a good assembly is to have a good story that pupils can relate to and then use it to focus on a symbolic message or moral.

Corridor patrol and lunch duties

The vast majority of schools will have senior management rotas for lunch duty and corridor patrols during the day. In these situations, you are expected to maintain a positive and light-hearted dialogue with pupils, whilst steering them firmly to their destinations. Duties like this can be highly stressful as 'crowd control' of large numbers of pupils can easily lead to chaotic or confrontational situations.

Doing corridor patrols safely and effectively

It is sometimes very difficult being the senior manager on patrol at lesson change-over or at the end of lunch time as one thousand or more young people move from one destination to another.

Even when the vast majority of pupils show no more than a good-natured physicality towards each other, issues arise which can put safety and professionalism on the line.

There may be typical low-level nuisance such as groups of pupils being very late getting to lessons, who seem to 'blank' you as you hurry them along. Then there are many varieties of body contact going on, much of it infringing other pupils' body space in an unhelpful way. Aggressive physical flirting, in which a girl squeezes a boy's arm or the boy runs off with a girl's bag. More unpleasant medium-level contact like holding another pupil in a full head-lock or strangling them – still a kind of horseplay. But these scenarios starting as jest can quickly escalate to a full-scale fight, which crowds of people gather around to watch. And the body contact tends to escalate as the school day nears its end. After lunch lessons seem to bring the pupils back to their lessons more restless and agitated than before. There is a ready-made recipe of difficulty for anybody involved in patrol. So what is the bottom line for us as senior managers. How does one deal with pupil physicality without being too physical ourselves?

The legal basis for teachers being physical with pupils lies in the 1996 Education Act and you must ensure you know this and the contents of your school policy and work within the guidelines. The Act allows teachers to use 'reasonable force' to prevent pupils doing any of the following: committing a criminal offence; injuring themselves and others; causing damage to property or engaging in any behaviour prejudicial to maintaining good order and discipline at school. But legal advice on what is 'reasonable force' is unclear beyond that force should be kept to an absolute minimum and will vary in each situation. My sense is that the law is most lucid dealing with physical restraint in the context of action necessary to stop injury to self and others. But it is much less clear cut where pupils are behaving in a way which compromises good order and discipline. When should you be physical with somebody to maintain 'good order' and 'discipline'? Stopping pupils attacking each other or a member of staff seems to be reasonable. But don't pull back a pupil trying to run down a corridor, block a pupil who tries to leave a room without permission or manhandle a pupil who has refused to leave a classroom.

The trouble is that 'shouting' or 'grabbing' are instant responses to defiance and disobedience. To avoid them is to defy intuitive human nature. Sometimes being professional means doing just that – ignoring your basic instincts.

Here is some advice on being physical and staying safe. Or better still, using alternative strategies to being physical at all. *Remember*: it is vital that you work within the guidelines of the 1996 Education Act and your school policy.

Using physical restraint

- Only intervene physically when your safety or that others is really threatened. Never intervene just to force somebody to follow your command.
- Try and keep you voice relaxed and calm. Keep the restraint to an absolute minimum. If you don't feel calm inside, don't intervene and simply don't touch the pupil.
- If you do get involved in an incident, write down the details of it immediately and give it to the headteacher.

Avoiding physical restraint

- 'Holding' or 'grabbing' are not illegal in most cases but are also likely to fuel confrontation. Sometimes it's better to pull back from an immediate confrontation and defer to follow up the pupils later.
- Follow-up can be by letter or phone call to parents. Pupils can be as confrontational as they like with you in the corridor or classroom, but if you refuse to rise to the bait, they can't stop you from contacting home later.
- Follow-up can take the form of going to a classroom and getting an individual away from a group of friends. Pick a time and place of your convenience and not theirs. Avoid being on your own with a pupil – get another member of staff to be with you.

More effective corridor patrols

- In the role of senior manager, accept that you will need to prioritise follow-up time after some corridor patrol situations.
- Don't expect instantaneous reaction when you give pupils a command. If you move away and give them time to hold onto their street cred before they obey you, your success rate will increase.
- Do corridor duties with other members of senior management. Working as a team is always a wonderful way to support each other and takes the tension out of many crowd-control situations.
- Humour always pays dividends. The more relaxed you stay, the more likely you'll be able to sort out a problem without becoming aggressive yourself.

Learning how to give an effective telling off

Senior managers have got to learn how to give a good telling off. They need to hone the skills they learned as a teacher and as a middle manager.

Deep in all teachers' subconscious is a primeval instinctive fear. It is something they dream of in the depths of the night. It is the nightmare scenario. And whether they are newly qualified or experienced, common pay spine, post-threshold or leadership scale, it's the same dream: losing control of the pupils. For a headteacher or deputy headteacher it might be losing control in a packed assembly hall or while supervising a lunchtime queue, for the ordinary teacher it's more likely to be with a difficult class, a cover lesson or between lessons, commuting from one room to another.

In the conscious world of school life this fear is greatest when their colleagues might be watching. As a senior manager you can take it as read that other teachers will stand back and watch how you manage a large group of pupils. As you enter the fray, be aware of your body visibly stiffening and the dangerous tendency to start barking commands like a regimental sergeant major on the parade ground. The inevitable result is confrontation, when it would have been so easy to avoid it. So how can you, a senior teacher, sidestep confrontation and win situations without explosions. Put simply, how can you give somebody a telling off without making a fool of yourself?

There is no easy answer to this question but the sensible rule of thumb is to accept that you will learn from experience and that means learning from your mistakes. However, there are things you could try that will make that learning experience shorter and a little less painful. It's important to learn a sense of timing. Some situations require a stern response. The pupils and your colleagues expect it from you. But you must be careful how you deliver it. It's much better to pick off individual pupils who challenge your authority and get them away from their peers – an audience they will be anxious to impress. Use your knowledge of the group. It's easier to pick off the most compliant individual, who is most likely to do as he or she is asked. One obedient student obeying you will encourage others to follow suit.

In a classroom or in a corridor situation, as has already been suggested, back off a bit after you've made a request. Pupils need a little time and space to 'save face' before they follow a command.

Watch your own body language as you give a command. Don't try aping the flamboyant or aggressive style of a colleague. There's nothing worse than copying somebody else and falling flat on your face. Try and keep your shoulders from tensing up and giving away the panic, inadequacy and frustration you might feel on the inside. It's always better not to shout but to repeat an instruction calmly but purposefully, while standing your ground.

You are likely to perform your telling off better if you keep a sense of humour and coax pupils along. Making light of a situation helps both teacher's and pupils' body language stay relaxed. This isn't the same as 'giving in' or condoning unacceptable behaviour. If a pupil continues to blank you and show complete dissent, warn them that there will be consequences for failing to follow your instructions. But it's best not to be too specific about what these consequences are as this could set you up for actions you find difficult to follow through.

Follow-up and consequences are a vital factor in any effective telling off. Follow-up takes the pressure off you to create an on-the-spot 'do or die' confrontation and win it. Through effective follow-up you can let a pupil disobey you, ignore you or simply storm off because you know you can find them later and deal with them.

So it follows on from that that you must always follow up pupils. Get them later that day or at the next available opportunity. When you meet up with them, it will be at a time of your choice and in circumstances that you've chosen and prepared for. Be prepared with the arguments you will use to take the moral, intellectual and emotional high ground. Come ready to take them away from their mates. Have reinforcements with you – a head of department, head of year, their tutor or another member of the SMT. It's very empowering to you for the recalcitrant pupil to see their teachers working as a team, and prevents you from being on your own with a pupil.

Top tips for telling off

1. Don't jump in feet first and stoke a big confrontation. You are just as likely to lose it as win it.
2. Follow up pupils who have been rude or defiant to you. This must be on your home ground and not on theirs. This will stop them playing to the gallery, their peer group audience. Instead, interview them in a quiet corridor or your office. If you can keep them waiting and keep them guessing about what might happen to them, this can be even more psychologically effective. One particularly effective technique is to come into their classroom and remove them. As they follow you out, they ask you if they are in trouble, to which you give no answer. They follow you down the corridor and you stay resolutely silent to all questions. The longer the walk, the more psychological tension is building up in the naughty pupil as they become increasingly anxious about their impending fate. Sit them down outside an office and leave them for ten minutes, to sweat over it.
3. Don't forget to follow up. If you don't, it's as bad as losing a confrontation. You'll lose your creditability in front of the pupils.

We will now look at the kind of highly confrontational situations to which you will be summoned, on emergency rota.

Emergency rotas

Other parts of your more generous non-contact time are also sucked into being on emergency rota during lesson time. The kinds of emergencies that crop up and their frequency during lessons times will vary greatly, depending on the kind of school you are in. The most common categories that get a request for a senior manager are:

1. A class is behaving so badly that the teacher feels they have lost control.
2. A fight has broken out in the class and the teacher needs help to separate the pupils and determine what the causes of the incident are and what the consequences should be.
3. A pupil loses their temper, either with the teacher or another pupil in the room. They refuse to leave the room or they leave the room only to keep on coming back into the classroom to disturb the lesson.
4. External intruders are spotted in the school.
5. Internal truants are hanging about in the corridors and disturbing lessons.
6. An incident occurs outside the school during lesson time that involves your pupils. Ones I have dealt with have included fighting in the street, shoplifting from a local shop or shouting abuse at local residents.
7. An angry parent comes up to the school and demands action. The most explosive confrontations occur when accusations of bullying by other pupils or unfair treatment from a teacher are the perceived issues. Sometimes parents blow their top when their child has been excluded for a time and they consider the punishment unfair. We will look at handling confrontations with parents in more detail later in this chapter.

Of the seven reasons listed above for call out, the most common type of emergency is when a pupil refuses to leave the room, often to go to the school designated punishment room.

Intervening effectively in pupil confrontations in the classroom

When you are called to intervene in these situation you never quite know what you are going to walk into.

Nine times out of ten, the appearance of a third party can break the deadlock in which a pupil is refusing to leave the room. But to be sure of success, the key is to enter into the confrontation of others, in a non-confrontational way. Rather than stride up to the recalcitrant pupil shouting, 'Your teacher has asked you to do something – now get on and do as you told!', ask them to come and talk to you outside, preferably sitting down beside them or bending down next to their desk to give them this instruction in a low voice. They will often be reluctant to go, because this means losing face in front of the class. Usually it is enough to reassure them that you only want to talk and they will get their chance to tell you their side of what went wrong. Saying this quietly, almost in a whisper, so that the teacher and the rest of the class can't hear, is likely to work best.

Failing that, I step outside the room and say that I will wait for them to do the right thing and join me. I deliberately walk away, giving them the time and space to take the option of following me out. It usually works, but nothing can ever be guaranteed. In extreme situations, where protracted violence is possible, I've asked the teacher to take the rest of the class out of the room.

On the very few occasions when a pupil has continually refused to leave the room, I've explained quietly that I am going straight off to contact their parents to ask them to take them home. This always has an effect, in so far as the pupil has finally accompanied me or stormed out of the room and run off. One way or the other, we have got a result in that the pupil is finally out of the lesson. Psychologically, the class have seen one teacher come to the assistance of another teacher and back up their decision. The departure of the pupil can be messy or clean but it has to happen, if the teacher wants it to happen.

Once out of the room, I will spend at least five minutes listening to what the pupil has to say for themselves in my office or at the very least in a quiet part of a school corridor. I have the luxury that the classroom teacher did not have: the time and space to listen to the problem properly in a busy lesson.

In these situations, I sympathise with the pupil as far as is possible and then try and get them to show empathy for the difficulties the teacher was having. Very often, a teacher has overreacted to what a pupil might have said or done, but the angry pupil hasn't appreciated that their individual lateness to the lesson or non-compliance with a simple instruction was the last of many irritating interruptions and the one that broke the camel's back. In the calm of my office, away from the audience of class-mates egging them on, many naughty pupils accept the scenario that you now explain to them.

I seldom send a pupil back to the lesson after such a confrontation has occurred, for fear of starting it up again. I often leave them to write up their side of the story or hopefully an apology note if they have come to accept by now that their behaviour was wrong. This gives the young person time to cool off and go on to their next lesson. Removal from class and a proper discussion of the incident is often sufficient punishment in itself, especially in situations when it is clear that both teacher and pupil have over-reacted. Often, I am taking a pupil out on the emergency rota to the 'time out' room. So the final part of my deconstruction of the event is to persuade them that they must accept the consequences of their actions and do their time in there. Then the incident will be truly finished with.

As a senior manager in volatile pupil–teacher scenarios, you must become sensitive and skilled at de-escalating situations that are already charged with anger and confrontation. You must learn how to unblock gridlock and produce a result by which both sides keep their dignity. Teacher and pupil alike need a compromise brokered which creates a 'win–win' situation. If the teacher has demanded that a pupil must leave a lesson, then the pupil must go. But afterwards it is important to bring the two sides together to negotiate a situation in which they can work together again. This can be done by the senior manager or delegated to a head of year or form tutor, but one way or another mediation is often necessary. In some less entrenched disputes, I advise a pupil to work out a solution for themselves. The suggestion is that they should find the teacher for a proper talk at the end of the day, when they are not surrounded by a difficult noisy class. Apologising for specific things that went wrong avoids saying sorry for everything that went wrong, some of it perhaps due to the teacher's overreaction. Taking the initiative, I suggest to the pupil, will almost certainly soften the teacher and put them in a conciliatory mood and will probably lead to an apology from them as well.

After an emergency rota scenario in which you remove a pupil, always get back to the member of staff to say what the final outcome has been. Face to face is better than writing a note, if you can find the time. It's an important part of the senior manager's role to reassure staff that they have been supported. It also creates an opportunity to talk about the difficult situation with the pupil or class and suggest some helpful solutions that the teacher may not have thought of.

The demand for a pound of flesh

You are often pressurised by staff who want to see naughty pupils 'hung, drawn and quartered' for their rudeness and defiance in the classroom. But often, as we have just seen, to solve a problem with a pupil who has just been difficult, it has been necessary to compromise on the punishment and mediate a 'win–win' solution for both pupil and teacher alike.

A significant group of staff will always frown on such compromise. They will argue that giving a challenging pupil a lighter punishment is pandering to their bad behaviour and letting them get away with it.

Arguments that help you justify compromise can be explained in the following ways: the pupil is very vulnerable and volatile and cannot function according to the normal boundaries of behaviour; punishment has to be imposed flexibly; punishment has already been given and consideration must be given for any recompense for actions that the pupil has made. At this point the difficult home circumstances that surround some pupils should be highlighted to encourage 'mercy' from hard-liners.

Restoring order to an anarchic class

Some emergency rota calls come about when a teacher is absolutely at their wits' end with the behaviour of the class. The level of disorder has brought them to personal meltdown and they call for help from senior management.

When one arrives in such a situation, the teacher is found struggling against the whole class, rather than one or two individuals. Even though the situation may have been of their own making, your duty is to help them regain as much control as possible to get the lesson back on track. This has to be done without completely undermining their authority in order to establish your own. The more disorder there is, the harder it is to stick to this advice. However, the following range of strategies are worth considering:

1 Stand beside, or slightly behind the teacher, saying nothing, while they call the class to attention and speak. This helps back them up, without taking the main authority away from them.

2 Walk round the room in a low-key way, telling individual pupils to be quiet and look towards their teacher. This will help your colleague gain control of the central stage again, without undermining them.
3 Pick on the most obviously poorly behaved pupils and take them out of the room with a big flourish. This may well give the teacher a window of opportunity for restoring order themselves.
4 Ask the teacher who has been misbehaving the most, and make a big display of taking them out with you. (This is a potentially risky strategy as the teacher's choice could ignite heated pupil protests, especially if he or she decides to name about ten people in the class.)
5 If the disorder looks too serious for the teacher to regain control on their own, it may be necessary to stand centre stage and wait for the class to be quiet. At that point, it is important to think of an intervention that will support rather than undermine the teacher and give them a chance to get back in the driving seat. I have discovered two practical strategies that work well. The first is to ask the teacher to give me a list of names of all the pupils who are good for the rest of the lesson. The second is a variant on the same theme. I ask the teacher to give the class a mark out of ten at the dismal moment I have arrived in the noisy room. I then tell the class I will return just before the end of the lesson and hope the teacher can give a mark closer to 10 out of 10. Both strategies encourage the teacher to build up a positive momentum again. On rare occasions, I give the class a dramatic moral lecture praising the skills and high levels of the teacher in the room. I almost always end by telling the pupils just how lucky they are to have somebody so experienced! It helps bolster the teacher's position and gives them another window of opportunity to teach.
6 Once a short intervention is made, it is important to leave the teacher to it, rather than hang around and wait for another deterioration in the lesson. The sensible teacher takes the help you have offered them and makes a real go at restoring order to the lesson. Others will get back into a silly confrontation from which it is almost impossible for you to help them again, other than to keep your promise to pop back in again before the end of the lesson.

Detective work and undercover investigations

One of the new skills you will need to learn when dealing with pupil behaviour at a senior level is how to mount a detective-style investigation. Only the former heads of year among you will be well versed in conducting interviews that lead to confessions. The kinds of pupil problems that lead to undercover investigations are:

- Pupils fight. Who, if anyone was to blame? Sometimes you need to call for eye witnesses to see who did what to whom etc.
- An act of vandalism – you will need to question witnesses in the vicinity or replay security camera footage if your school has it.
- A pupil accuses a teacher of assaulting them or vice versa.
- A group of pupils has attacked another pupil in the school building but nobody is owning up to it.
- There's been an incident on a bus or a train outside of school and you're trying to identify the group of pupils from your school that is involved.

Getting witness statements

A key strategy for the success of detective work is to pick on the weakest and easiest link in the chain. So if you are investigating a fight, question the least hard-bitten fighter first. Most fights have a rookie and a regular professional circuit-fighter involved – and the usual scenario is that the regular has picked on the rookie. It usually pays to follow this initial interview up by asking a couple of eye witnesses what happened. There is never a shortage of them at a fight. But the most reliable ones are not the people that the fighters can remember gathering around them, as they are often the friends or enemies of one or other of the combatants. They will lie to protect their friend or incriminate the enemy. But these partisan 'hangers on' can tell you the names of ordinary pupils just watching, who can give you the most useful evidence on how the fight started.

In most investigations, you need to get the information about what happened from another source, present it to the miscreants as 'game, set and match', so it reduces their chances of lying about it – the natural human reaction when one is in trouble.

In fights between two pupils, girls or boys, it's easy to get outrageously biased accounts from the two protagonists. Only the independent eye-witness reports establish who flung the first blow or whether a situation was more a case of one of the pupils viciously attacking another.

The hardest investigations to solve are when a pupil claims an assault by a teacher or when a group of pupils has been involved in attacking or robbing another pupil. Here, you can face more hardened and organised resistance to getting to the bottom of what really happened. Pupils who are already in trouble with the teacher will occasionally try and get out of it by saying they have been pushed or hit. But teachers do push and hit pupils in certain circumstances and deny it, and so this version of events can never be ruled out completely.

Effective interrogation techniques

Buddy detectives

For difficult investigations, which are going to take a lot of interviews and witness statements, it's useful to team up with a buddy detective – another member of the SMT. One of you takes the soft cop role and the other takes on the hard cop. As before, you go for the weakest link in the chain. The hard cop weighs in with a series of guesses about what the interviewee knows. After the hard cop has bluffed and implied that other people have already confessed to what they have done or what they saw, the hard cop threatens dire retribution on holding back on the truth. The argument usually used is that 'silence' will be taken as an assumption of full 'hands on' involvement in the crime. This can be enough to get a full submission but, if not, the hard cop leaves and soft cop enters. The soft cop deals with a bit of empathy and commiseration with the suspect, before outlining to them, in a very reasonable way, why it might be better to give in. The hard cop has concentrated on the moral high ground of the offence that the person has been accused of. The soft cop now gently but systematically goes over the details of the alibi again, looking for small inconsistencies.

All the protagonists are interviewed at different times and in different rooms, so they can't compare their stories. This leaves them lots of time to sit in silence and worry. Meanwhile the two buddy detectives regularly swop information and discuss tactics.

Use of film footage and other dirty tricks

As in the case of the kind of assault, robbery or intimidation that the police have to deal with, one of the biggest obstacles to senior management investigations getting to the bottom of something is that witnesses are fearful of giving information, for fear of reprisal in or out of school.

One regular trick that the detectives can use is to say that they have evidence recorded on film. Knowledgeable school villains are aware of where most of the school cameras are and will be at pains to wear hoods or scarves to hide their identity when in close vicinity to them. But they are never quite sure where all the cameras are, or if indeed there are some secretly concealed ones. When threatened with evidence from an unexpected source, they will often grass up a mate or admit to something themselves.

There are also ways of using cameras to give witnesses protection, while they are making positive identifications. I have got pupils to go to the room where the security cameras are monitored and then I've taken the suspect to select areas where the cameras beam onto. The witness can make an identification without putting themselves at risk. A variant on this theme is to lead the suspect into an area of the school where another pupil can identify them without being seen, such as looking down onto a playground from a classroom window or peering out of a room through a half-shut door into a corridor.

None of this would stand up in a court of law, where a witness usually has to make a statement with at least their name attached to it. But it is enough for a school investigation. At the end of the day, a senior manager detective does not need to prove a case to a judge and jury. Witnesses are mainly used to check the detail of a story and don't have to be named.

The key ingredients to a successful investigation

- Accept that unravelling an issue in which pupils are trying to conceal the truth from the school takes time. You must talk to a wide range of sources and collect and sift lots of detail.

Short-cutting this will inevitably lead you to make an unjust accusation or fail to gather enough evidence to proceed.
- The most effective investigations take place close to the event and not several days later. The bigger the time gap, the more the perpetrators have the chance to cover their tracks and prepare a collaborated story.
- An effective investigation always goes for the weakest and most pliable pupil first and tries to get them to tell the truth. But the central aim of pupil investigations must be to hear all sides of the story and get to the bottom of what really happened, as far as is humanly possible.
- Effective investigations are often best done as team work with the hard cop, soft cop approach.
- To get the information you need, you must think hard about how you will protect the identity of the eye witnesses. That's not too hard if there are lots of them, but much more tricky if there are only one or two.
- Be wary of witnesses who are partisan for or against the pupils involved in the investigation as they may be happy to lie to you.
- When you are not 100 per cent sure who did what to whom, give all involved a general warning that you'll be watching them and the investigation isn't over yet, even if later you drop it quietly. Don't jump to a potentially false conclusion. If you are accusing a pupil, a group of pupils or a teacher of a serious offence, then you must be absolutely sure of your ground. The surest way of creating bad blood with pupils, parents and teachers alike is to make accusations about wrongdoing that cannot be backed up.
- This doesn't mean to say you cannot pin a lesser charge on pupils. For example, you cannot prove that they stole a bicycle from the shed but you can prove they were truanting from their maths lesson.

The significance of good detective work to senior management

You might be asking yourself how my detailed descriptions of carrying out detective work on pupil misbehaviour can be a vital plank in building good relationships with the pupils themselves and their parents.

I would argue that being thorough and fair is one of the most important ways in which you build up respect as a senior manager in a school. When a pupil has been bullied and you show yourself capable of getting the evidence needed to stop it happening again, it reassures pupils and parents alike. There is no point being the kind of deputy headteacher who can devise a perfect assessment and reporting system, if you can't be bothered to give time to sorting out a bullying incident or the aftermath of a fight. Having said that, if your main responsibilities are curriculum based, you should usually go so far with investigation and follow-up, before passing it back to heads of year and pastoral SMT, who have much more detailed pupil/family knowledge to make a decision on what to do next.

Building relationships with the parents

In primary schools, the working relationships between parents and the school are much more regular. The children are younger and the parents can talk to the one class teacher about any problems when they collect them at home time. Even with this regular channel of communication, there can still be serious difficulties.

Communication with parents in secondary schools is much more difficult. The pupils are now old enough to come and go to school themselves so that the end of the day meeting slot disappears. And when a parent has a problem, there is no one class teacher to meet, only a bewildering array of subject specialists, all with their different teaching habits. The head of year and form tutor do not have the same level of familiarity with the teenagers in their care, spending much smaller amount of times with them. They will often be teaching when parental problems occur. As an assistant/deputy headteacher you will often be called on, in emergency, to deal with an angry parent who has decided to storm up to the school, out of sheer frustration with these complicated communication channels.

The vast majority of parents are very supportive of the school. But the parents who come unannounced seldom drop in to show this appreciation. They come up with a variety of complaints.

Parents in your average primary or secondary school are a very diverse group of people, with very different issues to let off steam about. Some are very pushy and intelligent and have come to complain about lack of homework or poor behaviour disturbing their son's or daughter's lessons. Then there are parents who will come to complain that their child is being bullied or has been truanting lessons and the school is doing nothing about it. Then there are parents who are convinced that one particular teacher is victimising their child. Some mothers and fathers come up to report that their son's or daughter's special needs are not being met and the teachers are going too fast in the lessons. Most of these problems are compounded by the fact that parents already feel that a subject teacher, head of year or tutor has not got back to them quickly enough. Because of the lack of opportunity for everyday informal meetings with the teachers, much more is reliant on leaving phone messages. But phone messages are not always listened to.

The most explosive trigger that brings a parent into the school without a pre-arranged appointment is the exclusion of their child. A letter arrives announcing that their son or daughter is now under their direct supervision during school hours for the next few days, bringing with it sudden and unexpected inconvenience to their own daily routines. They listen to what their child has to say about how unfair the exclusion is and then they steam up to the school to 'sort out the teachers!'

To pre-empt these kind of explosions, one of the senior management team needs to phone and explain the reasons for the forthcoming exclusion to parents. But getting hold of them before the event is not always possible because of the answering machine scenario. Exclusion letters are usually delivered in two different ways. The pupil is given one to take home by hand and one is sent by recorded post. For obvious reasons, it is often the second back-up copy that the parents get to see.

Disputed exclusions rely on the careful investigation work we have already discussed. So as a deputy headteacher, you'll have to hope that your fellow senior colleagues have understood the need to do a full investigation and keep proper written records. In an emergency call out, you may well find yourself trying to answer for the quality of work of another member of the team.

Dealing with an angry parent in the unexpected interview

When angry parents barge into a school and demand to speak to the headteacher, it is you rather than the headteacher who is likely to be called out. Nine times out of ten you are asked to respond to a situation where one of your colleagues or another pupil is being accused of having done something unfair to that parent's son or daughter. The priority as you meet the angry parents is to calm the situation, seek out more information on what the problem is, investigate those allegations with colleagues and get back to the family promptly.

Ten steps to pacify peeved parents

1 Don't begin your time with them by getting into a self-justificatory shouting match, defending the school's position. Get them out of the public reception area and into the nearest office.
2 Think of your body language and demeanour. Sit alongside the parents and lean forward to listen to their concerns rather than sitting officiously on the other side of the desk.
3 Let the parents have their say on the issues that they have a bee in their bonnet about. What they are most likely to be feeling is that nobody has bothered to listen properly to their side of the story at the school. Don't interrupt or interject. Just let it all spill out!
4 When they have got it out of their systems, you will probably still not know enough about the case directly to give them a detailed and informed answer to the issues raised. I usually summarise back to the parents at that stage what I think I have heard about the problem.
5 Promise that you will go away and check up on the facts. Usually this is the moment to ask a few questions to get more detail about what happened exactly. Taking deliberate notes also helps slow and calm things down. At this stage in the proceedings, I always remain completely non-judgemental about what has happened.
6 Explain what you are going to do next and the timescale for it. Give the parents a definite time when you will get back to them that day, even if it is only to touch base and tell them you've begun the investigation. Check their contact details and be sure to keep to your promise of phoning for a preliminary report-back.
7 Liaise with the staff and pupils involved in the situation. Depending on what has happened and your involvement in it as a senior manager, you will probably be able to delegate the

matter to the head of year or form tutor. Your experience of the staff and parents you are working with over a period of time will tell you when to fully delegate and when to hold onto the lead responsibility yourself. If the allegations are about staff abuse or maltreatment, you will have to consult the headteacher.

8 Whatever you decide to do, get back to the parents and explain fully what is happening. I would usually back this up by writing to the parents and copying it to the staff dealing with finishing off the work.

9 To give it that personal touch, make sure the parents know how to contact you directly again if the arrangements to solve a problem don't work out.

10 In all situations, try and broker a compromise solution that creates a 'win–win' situation. Parents need to feel they have been listened to and their opinions taken seriously. Teachers have to believe that they have been supported fully and fairly. Pupils need to appreciate that misbehaviour will have a just set of consequences attached to it and that negotiation between school and home will take place if they have been unfairly treated. Each situation is individual but it you stick to the ten steps listed here, you can usually defuse a difficult interview and bring about a positive result.

Chapter 8

Building relationships with non-teaching staff, school governors, the local authority and central government

In this chapter we look at:

- handling meal supervisors and premises staff and supporting them in their work, without being run ragged;
- the role of the governors in the school and how you can make the most of advice and questioning they can offer;
- surviving the onslaught of outside agendas from local authority and central government, by picking the best bits of the initiatives and using them to strengthen the priorities you have already identified for the school;
- presenting yourself as positive and upbeat to inspectors at all times.

Non-teaching staff

Secretarial support

The senior managers in a school often have line-management responsibilities that require a lot of memos, letter writing and reports. If you are to do your job well, you need effective administrative support from the school office. In particular, fast and accurate typing, as well as duplication and distribution to all the people who need copies. Good secretarial support like this increases your capacity to perform a number of jobs at the same time and can give your initial scribbles a real semblance of authority and efficiency.

Critical to this is asking your administrative support to save your files into carefully created folders on the computer so that you can find documents again when you need to repeat a similar activity a year or a month later and can no longer find your paper copy of it. As you are likely to be sharing secretarial time with other members of the SMT, it's all the more important to make sure that your personal work is retrievable quickly.

Meal supervisors

Senior managers do the lion's share of lunch duties and corridor patrols in most schools. This brings them into regular contact with meal supervisors. Whatever their training and experience, some meal supervisors seem to get into regular confrontations with pupils of all ages. A queue in a dining room is one of the hottest spots in the school day. Unless you work in an incredibly calm school, these queues can quickly resemble an angry mob on the first day of the January sales, with a sea of bodies pushing and shoving. Whether you stagger lunch hours or let many pupils off site to ease the pressure on your dining facilities, there always seem to be too many pupils trying to pass through the canteen.

Meal supervisors often try and demand the highest standards of behaviour from the pupils, far greater in their levels of insistence than teachers in a lesson. Indeed, they seem to despise large parts of the teaching staff, including some or all of the SMT for their lax, liberal standards. But their demand for good manners often backfires because they do not have the moral authority that comes from the positive relationships with pupils that teachers build in the classroom. So, whereas most teachers understand that the 'squaddie manner' doesn't work, some supervisors charge into confrontation, trading insults with the pupils.

Unfortunately when things go wrong, the meal staff expect the nearest senior manager to bail them out. And they don't respect your right to be off duty at that moment, trying to have your own short lunch break in peace, and instead drag you away from your mouthful, to get stuck into a shouting match. In fact, they are more likely to engineer a confrontation when they see senior management around.

Managing the lunch staff

1 Be nice to them and have a chat about things, in those quiet moments during lunch duty when everybody is relaxed.
2 Explain to individual supervisors, who constantly expect you to reinforce their authority, that you are not always on duty and are sometimes just getting your lunch. Therefore they should leave you alone, unless there's a real emergency.
3 Don't get drawn on the subject of pupils' terrible manners and behaviour. It's an invitation to a long commentary on how teachers and parents aren't strict enough, young people don't respect their elders and things weren't like this when they were at school. Given some of the meal supervisors are my age or younger, I know that the golden age to which they fondly refer never existed. I also appreciate that many of them truanted school themselves in their last years or now have children at this school or others who get into lots of trouble. They tell you this when they are feeling relaxed, but forget it when they have just had a confrontation with a pupil in the lunch queue. But it's not worth arguing with them, instead quietly note how intolerant one set of adults is of the shortcomings of many of the younger generation.

Strategies the SMT can use to control queues of pupils, especially lunch queues

- Organise the meal supervisors so that they are in position at least two or three minutes before a queue begins to form. It takes one minute to get the line of pupils in order and two minutes to block off all avenues for pushing in.
- If the queue starts in an orderly calm way, it's far easier to keep it like that. But if it's not supervised in the first couple of minutes and gets to be a seething mass of bodies, you will find it very hard to get order again.
- Ninety-five per cent of pupils will queue in a fair 'first come, first served' way, if there is order. Five per cent will try and queue jump. They will mainly be silly boys. If you stop them and ensure that they go to the back of the queue, everybody else will feel that justice has been done and will co-operate in adjusting the queue, if asked to.

- As a member of senior management, getting there to help the meal supervisors organise the first few minutes of the queue is the most effective use of your time. Once a pattern of calm is established, they won't need you anymore.
- If your arrive when the queue has got off to a bad start and is a mass of pushing bodies, the best intervention you can make is to form a human barrier by stepping somewhere into the middle and regulating the flow of people past you from that position. This won't be perfect but it will help restore some order for the lunch staff at the front of the scrum.
- Accept that when you or any other senior manager appears, people on duty stiffen up and if they are having confrontations with individual pupils, they will feel 'exposed' and will want to be seen to win the altercation. ' Winning' for some meal supervisors means getting an instantaneous response to their command from a challenging pupil. That is unlikely to happen! If the situation isn't going well, they will immediately request your support. Whereas, if you weren't there, they would find a way of sorting out the situation for themselves.

The premises team

Previously known as the school caretakers, some primary schools only have one who lives on the site. Big secondary schools could have a team of three of four people.

They are absolutely vital to the smooth running of the school, not just in school hours but for all the extended community use some primary and secondary schools have. As a senior manager, you need to call upon them in all kinds of urgent situations where their swift intervention will save you from protracted crowd-control problems. Many SMTs have walkie talkie or mobile phones that keep them in contact with each other and, most importantly, the premises team. Here's a flavour of the kind of issues you need their vital back-up for.

- A child has vomited all over the desk in the middle of the lesson.
- A pigeon is trapped in the stairwell of the main school building and pupils have gathered around, causing it to flap around in a state of panic.

- There's a dead mouse lying in the playground and a group of pupils have started kicking it around. A semi-hysterical mob has gathered around to participate.
- The sports hall needs to be converted from a large empty space into a 200-seater exam hall and back again to a sports hall in a 24-hour period.
- A window has been broken in a classroom door and there's jagged glass everywhere.
- Somebody has let off a stink bomb outside the headteacher's office, just before the chair of governors is due for a meeting on finance.
- A report that there is a burning smell in one of the bins on the second floor has come through.
- Lunchtime has ended and the playground needs to be cleared of litter before the local MP tours the building with the headteacher.
- Snow is on its way so the premises team needs to grit the playground. After it has fallen, they need to clear the playground of large pieces of ice, so that snowballing pupils cannot use them as dangerous missiles.
- A sticky drink has been spilled all over the main stairs. It's very slippery and needs to be cleared immediately, before lesson change.

This is a list of just some of the things they do, that make or break the good order of a school. Like the meal supervisors, the premises team are often very confrontational and 'macho' with the pupils. It is not surprising that they find them irritating when you consider the list of jobs I've just mentioned that they are regulary asked to respond to. They also bemoan the golden age when the pupils behaved respectfully and did not write graffiti, spit on stairs, drop chewing gum on the new carpet or flick cigarette butts behind the bike sheds. Yet, in those unguarded moments, they tell you how they personally did almost all of these things when they were larking around at school and got caned good and proper for it!

How to get the best out of the premises staff

1. Be pleasant and polite. When possible, give them plenty of warning of the jobs that you want them to do.

2 Consult them about the best way of doing something and try and come up with compromises that minimise hard work for them, whenever possible. This will mean that teaching staff don't always get everything they want.
3 Make sure you establish a clear system so that you or another member of the school office can contact them immediately if there is an emergency.

School governors

The headteacher has the main responsibility for working with governors. He or she will keep the right quota of governors on the full governing body and set up sub-groups on issues such as finance, staffing and curriculum. The senior managers, particularly the deputy headteachers (maybe assistant headteachers as well) will be asked to serve on one of the committee sub-groups. Most headteachers like having their senior management team around them in full governor meetings to reinforce their plans for the school with the outside audience and support them if the questions get very challenging.

What governors should do

A good set of governors will ask you intelligent, practical questions about the senior team's plan for the school. Their perspective as outsiders, on an issue, regarding the day-to-day running of the school can give you a fresh and sometimes very useful angle on the effects of what you are proposing to do. They may try and curb the most extravagant of your plans or at least make you dig deep to justify your intentions, which is good for you.

As a senior manager, it's very useful experience to work with governors, as preparation for being a headteacher yourself one day. In particular, try and sit in on the finance committee that sets and scrutinises the budget. This is one crucial area where a headteacher's role is very different from their senior managers in terms of that exclusive responsibility for a budget of millions. Seeing how it is done is the best opportunity you'll get for doing it yourself for real when you become a headteacher in your own school.

Local authority and central government relationships

Initiatives, initiatives, initiatives

One of the watch words for the new Labour government's spending from the late 1990s has been the phrase, 'Education, Education, Education'. 'Initiatives, Initiatives Initiatives' would be more apt. The following were initiatives in my school's Development Plan in 2003/4 in order to gain additional finance: Extended School Plan, Behaviour Improvement Plan, Education Action Zone, EC1 Regeneration Project, Key Stage Three Strategy, Leadership Improvement Grant, Pastoral Support Plan, Healthy School Action Plan, Citizenship Plan, Work-related Action Plan, Creative Partnerships, Excellence in Cities, Special Project to raise five A to C results and Information Technology Improvement Plan.

With such a range of initiatives, it is hard to see how any headteacher and SMT could find a way of prioritising work on them all in a way that would be helpful and efficient.

In addition to all this, a number of external organisations want to get into the school to do project work. Sometimes they offer their services for free, at other times they are looking to make money out of the school. Here is an example of a typical list.

- city banks offering mentors;
- lawyers wanting to run a human rights club;
- universities wanting to visit, to form partnerships and have groups of pupils brought to open days;
- Shakespearean actors running Macbeth workshops;
- local authorities' SATs booster classes in maths, English and science;
- Howard League for Penal Reform wanting to do Year 8 workshops;
- Skills Force, a government-funded organisation, working on Year 10 vocational courses;
- external enrichment classes for able and gifted students on journalism at the City University;
- Hugh Masekela teaching students to sing African songs, ready for a concert he is planning;
- Speak Up, Speak Out, a public-speaking organisation running classes in Year 9;

- an environmental project working with pupils to redesign the playground.

This is a drop in the ocean when you see just how many other organisations regularly mailshot or phone schools looking for business. The senior management team have to co-ordinate all this potential activity and plan the daily school diary so that the extra-curricular offer doesn't become too burdensome.

Everybody wants to get in on the act and have a piece of the action in schools. Yet there is little proof that many of these short interventions make any real difference to the pupils' real educational chances and some may get in the way of concentrating on key learning objectives in regular timetabled lessons. The bewildering array of initiatives, visitors and advisers is so confusing that a senior management team could spend their whole time servicing these 'bit part' players, rather than get on with prioritising their own school improvement agenda.

Working with the local education authority

To determine your own agenda as a school leader, you have to be ruthless about moulding these external agendas to specific actions within your line-management remit and educational vision of how to improve the school. The local authority has now become the gatekeeper for many of the central government's educational initiatives and spending streams. Without this role, the very existence of LEA advisers and inspectors would be in doubt. The local bureaucracy is constantly pressing you to implement things that the government has set up. Some of these initiatives are genuinely useful but others are half baked. Most have something good in them and prioritising that specific bit of the initiative that fits in with your current plans for the school is a sensible course of action. Unfortunately, LEA officers also dream up borough enrichment activities and extension classes without consulting two vital interest groups properly: teachers and pupils. As a result of this, you are expected to sell an idea to pupils and staff that they have no ownership of and consequently no interest in implementing.

Your headteacher may need to work closely with the local authority and this will limit your ability to opt out of all their 'pie in the sky' schemes. Headteachers who work in schools with high exam results and a relatively motivated pupil population have as much contact with the LEA as they choose to. It is schools in challenging circumstances that are pressurised into spending lots of time with local authority advisers, who insist on supporting them as 'critical friends'. This includes setting challenging targets for improvement every year. This means that valuable time in your working day can be squandered, justifying your actions to local authorities, setting targets that are artificially high, writing unnecessary additional action plans and accounting for your use of small extra funding streams. It can become a constant battle to cherry-pick the best initiatives on offer and fit them with your own key issues.

Central government

Central government initiatives often drive the local authority agendas. In recent years this has been true of national strategies on literacy and numeracy.

But central government also has a vast array of additional initiatives, which it bypasses local authorities to put directly into schools through Standards Funding. If you are a senior manager involved in producing student data, a significant amount of your time will be sucked into presenting statistics to central government, so that they can reproduce comparative league tables of school performance and value-added analysis. If your senior management remit includes social inclusion, a vast network of external behaviour management advisers, social workers and psychologists are now working in a multi-agency way in your school. This often looks better on paper than it works out in practice. Again, valuable time can be swallowed up with a quagmire of paper, meetings, bids for funding streams and a lot of confusion as to who is accountable for what.

Dealing with external organisations

1 Try to prioritise some of the local and central government initiatives passed on by the headteacher to you. Ignore some of them by putting them quietly to one side. Make a minimum effort with others.
2 Take the best of the initiatives and mould them into a shape that fits in with something you have already made a priority

in your job description. Remember that not every suggestion can be a priority, otherwise the word 'priority' becomes meaningless.

3 Spend as little time as possible with poor advisers and organisations, but try to fight your natural instinct to tell them to 'get lost' and stop wasting your precious time.
4 Use the good advisers and good organisations or the good people in bad organisations as much as you can. You will know who they are when they offer to do something practical alongside teachers in the classroom. The poor advisers show their colours when they start pestering you to fill in bits of paper and don't want to spend time in lessons with pupils.
5 Remember that working with your local authority and central government is a balancing act. They want you to be fond of them and try all the latest educational wheezes for improving standards. But if you try too hard to please them, you might never get round to sustaining your own priorities for making the school a better place. So be nice to them, take their funding, but divert the resources to actions that you have already prioritised.

Working with the inspectors

Inspectors come and visit you in the school from the local authority and central government. They need to be treated with extreme caution. If we lived in an educational world where there was open dialogue, inspectors would be trusted to take the truth back to the educational masters about the real challenges facing your school and how you are dealing with them. But often it seems that inspectors focus on any weaknesses you admit to and then blame them on inefficient leadership and management in your school – so what's wrong will become your fault! This encourages headteachers and senior teams to 'spin positively' at any opportunity and put on a never-ending 'good show' to external audiences. The current system of punitive inspection unfortunately encourages you to 'talk up' rather than 'talk about' problems.

How to handle inspectors effectively

1 Be polite and attentive. Frame your comments positively. Give everything you are in charge of 'the sun ray treatment'. So something that clearly isn't working is described in terms of 'it would be even better if'.
2 Prepare yourself carefully for an inspector's visit, in the same way as you would for a job interview. Think through what you have done and find the evidence for it. Practise describing all your work in a very positive light so that the glass is described as 'half full' and not 'half empty'.
3 Give the inspectors paper records of the progression of an initiative. They love documentation that justifies what you are saying.
4 Don't ever complain about the inefficiency of other organisations, agencies or individuals. Honest evaluation of the work of others could bounce back on you. Keep the real evaluation for what is working and what's not for senior management discussions and, with a little more circumspection, for your governing body.
5 Getting a good inspection report always reinforces your position as an effective senior manager. It will empower you to get on with the issues you have identified as important in the school. A thumbs-up from the inspectors is a seal of approval, even if the truth about what you really do well has not been appreciated or even mentioned. A bad report will lead to inevitable questions about your efficiency and self-presentation skills. This will not help your standing as a manager in the school.

Of course, positive spin ultimately confuses the issue of what is really good and what is a problem. But this is the world in which senior managers have to exist. It is a world in which politicians set targets for education, which again and again are not met, perhaps because they are setting the wrong targets in the first place. The political masters, whatever their party politics, seem uncomfortable with the day-to-day realities of disruptive behaviour and low educational standards of literacy and numeracy from a significant minority of pupils in our schools. They want to wish away the disorder in the corridors as rowdy exuberant teenagers pass from one lesson to another. Instead, schools are forced into a mode where they have to be continually upbeat about all the challenges they face. If you are a part of a senior management team, you need to understand this agenda and respond to it effectively. But this shouldn't stop you celebrating your many real successes – the ones that the inspectors don't necessarily ask you about or think important.

Part 3

Developing essential skills and survival strategies

Chapter 9

Managing change

In this chapter we look at:

- key factors for managing change effectively;
- the features of your management style that you need to develop in order to be a positive change manager;
- a case study of what can go wrong with a plan to develop the curriculum;
- a case study of more effective curriculum development;
- how to conduct an effective evaluation.

Change in schools comes from both the inside and the outside. It can be the result of the educational vision of a new headteacher or the new political dogma of a government.

Demographic changes outside a school's control such as falling birth rate can lead to its complete reorganisation. Competition from a new school in the area can affect the quality and quantity of pupil intake. Every era of education has new school initiatives – there are always three or four major initiatives in the field of vision at any one time. Underlying all these incremental initiatives are slow transformational changes in the society in which we live, impacting on schools. The education system links to the changing employment market and this is an increasingly technologically based enterprise culture in which job security is minimal and flexible skills are vital. This puts pressure on the curriculum to change and adapt.

Even if the government did not try and control the direction of schools and the headteachers did not implement their ideas, change would occur naturally with staff coming and going from a school community through retirement and promotion. As a senior manager, you have to become competent at handling a continuous flow of change and development, encouraging yourself to work in the following ways:

1 *Be proactive*: to be an effective senior manager, you have to use your initiative to influence the change that is going on around you in a positive self-enhancing way.
2 *Be flexible*: you need to be able to adapt to the demands that new situations can bring. In my current school in the last three years, each year has brought big changes. For the first year I was the assistant headteacher in charge of inclusion and the school special needs co-ordinator. In the second year, as a deputy headteacher, I took on student data analysis and exam line management. In the third year, I dropped most of the inclusion role, including special needs co-ordinator and assumed a main-stream curriculum base. My office was moved from one side of the building to the other. In the next eighteen months the school could become a city academy, admitting a wider age group of pupils (5–18) onto a split site, whilst merging with a specialist school for children with significant physical difficulties. With such changes, my role, office space and general daily life will be radically affected again.
3 *Be imaginative and creative*: all the change I have just described in one school offers many opportunities to be imaginative and creative. Your job in senior management may not change as much as mine has, or will, over the next three years but, mentally, you need to be the kind of person who sees opportunities in new situations.

Attitudes to change

Management styles that encourage effective change and development

An effective manager:

- acts
- sees opportunities in difficult situations
- has breadth of vision
- takes responsibility for their actions

- analyses a problem objectively
- listens and responds constructively to issues raised by other staff
- proposes solutions to problems
- delegates to others
- will confront the source of the problem
- learns from difficulties and past mistakes
- has foresight.

Management styles that discourage effective change and development

An ineffective manager:

- is a victim of circumstances
- blames others for things that go wrong
- takes a subjective rather than an objective viewpoint when trying to solve a problem
- rejects suggestions on how to solve a problem
- criticises without offering alternative solutions
- is unlikely to delegate
- sees the potential threat in any change
- is preoccupied with detail
- conceals problems (maybe by talking them up through positive spin)
- talks about the source of the problem, but doesn't act to do anything about it
- looks back, with hindsight.

Most managers are a blend of positive/proactive and cautious/reactive

There are situations when a blend of proactive and reactive leads to the successful management of change. For example, it is often productive to use hindsight as well as foresight to improve the way you do things. Whilst it is a good thing to see opportunities in difficult situations, it is also important to work out details properly and not to rush into a development. A good manager is also sensitive to the fact that human beings usually fear sweeping innovations and some difficult situations are best compromised on, rather than tackled head on.

A case study illustrating how to manage change badly

Sarah wanted to get off to her holiday cottage for the weekend. There was just the staff meeting to deal with. It was her fourth year as headteacher of a comprehensive school – four years of finding out just how 'intransigent' and 'unimaginative' the teachers could be. It seemed to her that they were always moaning and complaining about their conditions of work and the behaviour of the children. Every year, as far as she could remember, there was always a big debate about how the Year 7 started out angels in early September, but had turned into monsters by Christmas.

One day in June Sarah was struck by the perfect scheme to sort out Year 7 once and for all! There was still half a term of the summer left and the timetable wasn't fully completed. Still time to change the curriculum and the staffing model for next year.

The first three items on the staff meeting agenda had not gone that well and there were only fifteen minutes left when they got to the issue of Year 7. People had been shuffling in their seats and muttering to each other, but now she began to explain her plan to keep the new Year 7 'calm'. An uneasy, almost deathly silence fell over the meeting. Sarah proposed the 'zoning' of Year 7. The young ones would stay on one corridor of the school and have their subject teachers come to them. It would feel like a primary school, each group having its own dedicated classroom. She also declared that it was her aim to change the timetable so that the English department could teach humanities as well, giving them up to eight hours with each Year 7 class. This was as close as they could get to having a primary-style teacher in the classroom. By doing all this Sarah was sure that the Year 7 would stay unsullied for longer, set apart from the rest of the school by her newly proposed arrangement.

When she had finished, lots of hands shot up. The senior management did not join in, out of deference to her, but they also looked worried and surprised. She had briefed them on the outline of her plan for just two minutes that morning in the SMT meeting. The questions started. 'Why don't you get more senior management patrols on the corridor, instead of changing everything for the whole of Year 7?' 'Year 7 are no worse than Year 8 or Year 9.' 'Do you seriously think that having teachers moving around to the different Year 7 classes, carrying all their stuff in a box is going to improve the behaviour in the lessons? Surely, it will make the teaching worse?' This last question was an objection she had not thought of, but it was taken up and echoed by other teachers as a major stumbling block to the plan.

Then, the current head of Year 7 pointed out that if Year 7 was going to be zoned, some teachers would lose their own teaching classroom. 'Which department will have to move to make way for the Year 7 zone?' asked another teacher. Sarah had to admit to the meeting that she had not decided on this implication of her plan. Then one of the English teachers interrupted: 'I came to this school to teach English, not RE or history.' There was no answer to this question or others such as: 'Why haven't we had a chance to discuss it?' and ' What's the point of all this change?'

Where has Sarah gone wrong?

Her objectives were not fully recognised or understood

Nobody was quite sure where Sarah's idea had come from. She saw the zoning of Year 7 as solving problems to do with discipline, but was this the real cause of the deterioration in the year group's behaviour every year? Did it really matter that they moved lessons or that they had lots of subject teachers. There had been no proper discussion of these issues. It felt as if Sarah was acting on her own hunch or whim.

She hadn't prepared the ground for her changes

Sarah had plucked the solution for the problem of Year 7's problem out of the air. She was attempting to rush something through and was cutting corners. There had been no proper discussion of the issues upon which to structure such a major change. The only person with any kind of ownership of the plan was the headteacher herself.

Sarah had not consulted properly

None of the staff had been consulted about Sarah's brainchild. People's first reaction was to see how her changes would affect them personally. Many felt threatened, realising that they would lose their teaching room or parts of their subject specialist teaching timetable. These were big and immediate personal issues.

No details of the plan were available in advance

There was nothing to read and cogitate over before the meeting. This added to people's anxiety. Sarah had not left sufficient time in the meeting to have a full discussion of all the issues raised. The zoning item was the last one on the agenda.

The staff didn't respect Sarah's management

Judging by the tension and angry reaction to the plan, the teachers did not have unquestioning respect for Sarah or her SMT. They did not feel confident that she had a track record for handling 'change' effectively. Perhaps they would have listened more willingly if the headteacher had already taken them through successful changes before.

The plan did not convince

Because she had thought the plan up quickly, without running her ideas past any of her colleagues, lots of potential objections to it had not been discussed and solutions worked out in advance. The staff came up with a whole series of worries and objections that Sarah had not thought of. She, after all, did not rely on keeping her teaching resources in her own classroom. She only realised the problem of a subject area losing its dedicated space when somebody had questioned her about it in the meeting. Yet the practicalities around the 'what abouts' or the 'what ifs' were essential in giving the staff confidence that she knew what she was doing. More and more people could see that the whole idea was poorly worked out. This made confidence drain away from the plan even more quickly.

Factors affecting successful change

1. The content of the 'change' needs to be carefully worked out step by step in order to take the school from A to B.
2. People affected by the change need to be communicated with fully about what is happening and why.
3. Proposed changes may need modification; those affected often raise objections that need to be accommodated.
4. Teachers need to be convinced that 'change' is needed, otherwise they will refuse to take ownership, actively or passively.

5 Each change needs to assimilated so that new ways of doing things are properly consolidated into the routines of a school. Otherwise there's a danger that the changes will simply peter out.
6 Change often works best in small practical steps, not in one big jump. Each step needs to be evaluated carefully before going on to the next one.
7 If you are already in an institution where there has been successful change in the past, it's likely you can repeat the experience.

Qualities to expect in a good change manager

- They know what they are trying to achieve.
- They explain it clearly to others.
- They can back their desires up with a practical plan of action.
- They can present the change as personally rewarding for a lot of teachers and pupils.
- They are comfortable with bringing in change that incorporates the viewpoint of other members of staff and not just their own.
- They question the need to do something in the way it has always been done.
- They keep going and stay positive in the face of some setbacks.
- They are pragmatic and plan flexibly, making the best use of available resources.
- They move forward one step at a time and don't rush ahead too quickly.
- They have a record of making successful change happen.
- They are prepared to back off when they realise that a change has not been properly thought out and apologise to the staff for causing them anxiety.

Managing curriculum change

As a senior manager you are most often asked to plan and implement a curriculum change of some kind. This could be as a result of an internal plan agreed by senior management or because your school has to implement a government directive. Whatever type of curriculum development you are planning, it is certain to involve the way your staff are deployed to work.

Introducing master classes for gifted and talented pupils: a case study of curriculum development

Introducing day-time master classes for the most able students

Over the last eight years, the Labour government has funded inner-city schools with a substantial additional budget for the top 10 per cent of their pupil intakes. The young people, identified as gifted and talented, are supposed to receive a richer curriculum to encourage them to stay in difficult urban schools. I have been in charge of this initiative and have sought to find strategies to make an impact with this extra funding. In my school this has been about £18,000 pounds a year.

The government had always said that they want the money spent on making the daily classroom experience of the most talented pupils better, rather than spending money on after-school enrichment opportunities. But it is very hard to change the quality of top-set teaching across all the subjects in the school, when the vast majority of teachers gravitate to planning for the middle ground in the top sets and not the very highest of abilities. Obviously, one way of spending the budget was to train teachers to differentiate their materials more effectively, but I decided to prioritise the course of action suggested from the extensive pupil evaluation I conducted.

The gifted and talented pupils said that they wanted to be taught in smaller groups, where disruptive behaviour didn't exist. Even top-set lessons in inner-city schools can suffer from off-task behaviour. The pupils wanted their regular teachers to take these special lessons during the normal school day and not as twilight enrichment activities. I nicknamed the provision they were asking for 'master classes'. Although the pupils' evaluation of what they wanted had been very clear, I did not know what the teachers' response would be. I decided to proceed with the master classes concept by using the faculty monitoring programme I am in charge of to introduce the idea to teachers. I made teaching and learning for the top 10 per cent the theme for monitoring in the highest sets. Having watched top-set lessons, I spoke to individual teachers about master classes. The key selling point for running one was that they would have an incredibly rewarding experience with a small group out of their regular top set and could experiment with teaching content and pedagogical styles that they wouldn't normally use in a big mainstream lesson. The master class would be a place to rehearse new things, many of which could be modified and taken back to the regular top-set lessons. My master-class initiative began as two pilot days with four teachers from languages. They were quite happy to give it a try, but their initial experiences raised some key issues.

1 What would happen to the rest of the class while the teacher had a small number out on a master class?
2 What about the length of the master class – should it be the usual one-hour lesson or longer?
3 What about the time factor involved in preparing master classes?
4 Should there be any extra payment involved for teachers participating in the programme?

As my programme spread to other faculty areas, I found that the maths faculty preferred to do the master class in their own non-contact time, rather than leave the remainder of the class with a supply teacher.

The implementation of the initiative taught me how important it was to evaluate the experiences of both pupils and teachers every step of the way. When people had strong feelings about the length of master classes, I simply accommodated their wish for longer lessons. Having seen a variety of different ways of running master classes, I reported back to the headteacher and the SMT about the practical issues of running them throughout the school. The issues of equal opportunities for the rest of the pupils, extra payment for teachers and the length and frequency of the classes came up in this forum.

The gifted and talented master-class initiative demonstrated a number of important points about managing curriculum change effectively.

Key considerations for successful curriculum change

1 Some curriculum changes move fast and others slowly. The plans that you prepare need regular adjustment and evaluation. Don't ignore initial feedback and press on as before. In the case of the gifted and talented master classes, movement

was slow and teachers brought up important concerns at each stage.

2 Break a complex task down into manageable chunks. For example, it would have been far too difficult to introduce master classes across every faculty in the school at once, much better to experiment with their introduction in one subject area, in this case modern languages and learn from their experiences.
3 Any major curriculum change revolves around the management of people, not of tasks. If the staff come up with problems, you need to try and address them. For example, the gifted and talented master classes raised big issues of equal opportunities. What would the experience of pupils left out of the master classes in the room with a supply teacher be? Many subject teachers we asked to participate were very concerned about this.
4 Build on 'enthusiasm' and seek to pass ownership for the way an initiative unfolds to the teachers themselves. If the majority are reluctant about what you are proposing, the plan is unlikely to be successful. But when there are some differences, compromise is usually possible so that the plan evolves in a way that allows every individual teacher a slightly different formula for success. For example, some of the language teachers wanted more than one-hour master classes. One wanted to hire costumes and buy in props for a whole morning in the hall. This was far more elaborate than I had envisaged as the norm, but the teacher was so enthusiastic that I decided to give them what they wanted. On the equal opportunities issue, opinion was divided. Some staff were prepared to accept the compromise of taking one half of their top set in a master class this term and the remainder next term. Others weren't worried about taking out the very brightest pupils from the top set and two teachers declined to participate in master classes because of this problem.
5 Don't try and skimp on the resources for a major curriculum change. Allow additional resources and time for people to work together or to train. At present, no payment has been agreed for preparation or delivery time for gifted and talented master classes. The headteacher's opinion, at the moment, is that there is no case for these payments. The pilot groups have accepted it, but if I thought that the groundswell of opinion from the teaching staff was that they wouldn't do master

classes unless they got extra pay, then I would strongly recommend to our headteacher that he change his mind rather than lose the momentum of a very good teaching project. Luckily, the Workforce Remodelling Agreement might create new ways of getting staff to run gifted and talented master classes at times of the year when they would have normally have been invigilating public exams.

6 Don't create an 'in favour ' group in the school that get all the patronage. Share out the 'opportunities' amongst every one. In the case of the master-class initiative, it has been extended to one faculty after another. When one languages teacher got missed the first time round, she got her master class included on the second pilot day.
7 Keep all the staff in the school up to date about how the curriculum development is going. This maintains a high profile and encourages other departments to come on board. For example, all the work around the gifted and talented master classes has been publicised in the weekly bulletin. The evaluation of the pilot days in one faculty has been passed on to the others.
8 Vital to measuring the success or failure of the initiative is to make sure you conduct an effective evaluation. This is the part of the process that busy schools are most likely to forget to do properly. Often all the effort and energy is put into the implementation of a curriculum change and the evaluation of success or failure never takes place.

Action planning curriculum change

Build up your plan around these vital questions:

- Where are we now?
- Where do we want to go?
- How are we going to get there?
- What will it cost?
- What are the training needs of the staff involved?
- How shall we know when we have achieved our main objectives?

Evaluation

There are many ways to measure your success with a curriculum development. For an evaluation method to work, you need to be sure of what you are trying to evaluate. This means asking the right questions.

Key methods available to carry out evaluations

You could use just one or a combination of the following evaluation techniques:

- analyse the action plan itself: What goals did it set itself? Which goals were met as a direct consequence of the planned action? Which goals came about as an indirect spin-off?
- written evaluation: a questionnaire for those in involved in setting up and running the initiative;
- group discussion with the teachers involved in the initiative
- individual interviews with the teachers involved, formal or informal;
- interviews with the pupils;
- classroom observation of the initiative being implemented;
- written work sampling, to look at the effect that the initiative has had on the pupils' mind-set;
- on some occasions you might ask a member of staff who has had nothing to do with the initiative to evaluate it so as to avoid the danger of bias and positive spin.

A typical and simple format for all types of evaluation would use the following questions:

- What is going well?
- Have all parts of the curriculum development been equally successful?
- How far have the original objectives been met?
- What adjustments to the programme would be sensible?

Chapter 10

Key communication skills for senior managers

In this chapter we look at:

- oral presentation to varied stakeholders such as teachers, parents or governors;
- written communications with all the staff and parents;
- running large- and small-scale meetings with the staff, parents and governors;
- leading a school for varying periods of time as the acting headteacher.

Oral presentations

Many of the preceding chapters highlighted the importance of communication skills in small-group or one-to-one situations with staff, parents and pupils. But 'putting on a show' in front of large groups is also a vital skill for a senior manager. We saw in Chapter 7 that giving an entertaining assembly will impress the pupils and raise your standing with them in crowd-control situations in corridors. Teachers are also impressed by a good assembly, but they need to see your eloquence in a much wider variety of situations such as running a staff meeting or chairing a large curriculum committee.

Although most senior management selection processes have already assessed your potential for presenting ideas to a large group of people, there is always room for improvement in this vital field.

Different ways of delivering presentations

There are a number of ways to speak to large groups of the staff and each has advantages and disadvantages:

1 You could write it out what you want to say, word for word and then read it out. This is the safest method of delivering a speech because your lines are always there and you can't go wrong. But lack of body language and particularly eye contact will pack no punches with the audience.
2 You could write it out and memorise it. This allows you to use a lot of eye contact with the audience. Speaking without notes will make you look very knowledgeable and self-confident. But when you're nervous, it's easy to forget what you wanted to say. Also, memorising a long speech eats up valuable time that you could be spending getting on with the rest of your busy job description.
3 You could write the main ideas onto an overhead projector or give a PowerPoint presentation. This reminds you of what you want to say, as well as providing visual stimulation to your audience. With key words and phrases to refer to, you will feel more confident to fill in around your prompts, still giving your audience a lot of eye contact and attention. There are no obvious disadvantages to this method, unless you are too nervous to ad lib around the key words or phrases.
4 You could do a presentation 'off the cuff'. This can generate a lot of excitement and freshness through its spontaneity. It can capture a moment. But the disadvantage is that it leaves you vulnerable to nerves. A carefully prepared viewpoint is much safer when the pressure is on. An ideal scenario would be to make the highly prepared presentation sound so fresh and spontaneous that it comes over as 'off the cuff'.

Preparing your message to make maximum impact

- What are the critical points you want to communicate in this presentation? If you were able to ask somebody in the audience to summarise those issues, what would you hope they would repeat back to you?
- Pitch your speech to the audience. Pupils are different from

teachers, teachers from senior managers, parents from governors. This means thinking carefully about language, jargon, level of detail and presentation of statistical data.

- Try to begin with something that gets your audience's attention such as a controversial or colourful opinion to wake them up or a school scenario that you know will ring true for them.
- Humour can give that informal and intimate touch to act as an ice-breaker in various parts of the presentation, especially to relax the listeners at the beginning.
- Even if you are trying to persuade your audience of a particular argument or course of action, give both sides of the case to show you are not trying to stack the cards flagrantly with a 'hard sell'.
- Use some good visual aids, but don't bombard your audience with them. Four OHP or PowerPoint slides are plenty for a ten-minute talk. Don't write too much on them as it can't be read properly at a distance.
- Keep it short: fifteen minutes or so of you talking and people listening is sufficient; after that people's attention begins to wander. If you are running a longer training session, you need some activities to take the audience away from you at this point, so that they interact amongst themselves.
- Leave time for plenty of questions as the audience get very annoyed if they don't get the chance to have their say.

I include at this point the Top Ten Tips for speaking published by Speakers Bank, an organisation that arranges public speaking training in schools and the workplace. These points make good sense for any school senior manager trying to communicate effectively to their staff.

Top Ten Tips for speaking in public (published with the permission of Speakers Bank, www.speakersbank.co.uk)

1. Be yourself: as a speaker it is you they want to hear from – your views, your stories, what you think should be done, your interpretation of the facts.
2. Structure your talk: your audience needs an outline or framework to help them follow what you are telling them. Make sure it has a clear beginning, middle and end.

- Opening: you need a strong start to attract audience attention. Issue a challenge, state an issue, give a quote, ask a question.
- Body: have no more than three key points to your talk.
- Conclusion: finish confidently and with conviction – a call to action, a challenge or a question.

3. Eye contact: maintain eye contact with your audience at all times – even when you are thinking about what to say next.
4. Speak from the heart and with passion: real conviction breeds enthusiasm. If you are listless or half-hearted, they will be too. Your commitment is your greatest asset. They need to see, hear and feel what you are telling them.
5. Keep it simple: tailor your speech to your audience. It is about what they need and want to know, not about how much you can tell them.
6. Remember the power of the pause: in speechmaking the power of silence can greatly add to the impact of your talk. Try it!
7. Use your voice and your body: gestures and vocal variety (pitch, pace, pause and volume) enhance your performance.
8. Speak to time – don't go on for too long: give your points and then sit down.
9. Practise. Practise. Practise. Try it out in front of a mirror at home – it really helps. Get feedback from your friends/boss or family members.
10. Speak up! and Speak out! project your voice to the back of the room. Your voice needs to be heard – never say no to a speaking opportunity.

Handling questions

Teaching staff, parents and governors will expect you to be self-confident at answering their questions after you have made a presentation to them.

- Make sure that your audience understand in advance how you intend to deal with their questions: are they free to interject as you present your case or do you want them to save questions for the end?
- When questions are asked, repeat them for every body's benefit in as loud a voice as it takes, for everybody in the room to hear.

- If you're not sure what the question is getting at, ask for clarification rather than stumble into an answer.
- Don't let a single questioner or question dominate, even if you decide to pursue a question through several more supplementary questions and answers.
- Avoid getting sucked into a long wrangle over one point and don't get pulled into a personal confrontation in which you start interrupting the other speaker.
- Be sure to distinguish between what is your personal view and what is school policy.
- Try and make eye contact with the whole audience, even when you are answering one person's question.
- Remember, your body language is telling your audience how relaxed and self-confident you are feeling, whatever you are actually saying.
- If people are chatting or going off on their own discussions, ask them politely to return to the task and pay attention. But try and keep it light.
- Keep your answers to the point and don't repeat yourself endlessly.

Drafting documents

Senior managers in schools are constantly communicating by written word as well as speech. The audience for their writing includes parents, local authority bureaucrats, teachers in the school and fellow senior colleagues. To write effectively, you need to communicate in a large range of writing styles such as:

- discussion papers, outlining key points of an issue from a number of standpoints;
- information sheets that brief staff about events or educational matters;
- reports on the activities of a working party or evaluations of initiatives;
- funding bids in which you construct proposals to get money for the school;
- action plans, which propose courses of action and rationales with short-term and medium-term goals, explaining how success will be measured and who is responsible for seeing them through;

- letters to parents (behaviour matters, health matters, congratulation letters and educational matters).

Tips for effective written communications

- As with a meeting you are chairing or oral presentation you are giving, know what you want to write and how you wish to get your main point over to the audience.
- Make it easy to read, with ideas broken down into simple language and as little jargon as possible.
- Summarise the main points at the end of each section. If it's a longer paper, use bullet points.
- Make clear what the key dates for action are and who is responsible for taking that action by putting these in bold type.
- If you are writing a letter with unpalatable information to parents about their son or daughter, keep the language as neutral as possible and try to offer something supportive, to help them deal with the bad news you are giving them. For example, mentioning something positive about the pupil to counterbalance the strongly negative sound of the letter.

Managing meetings

One-to-one line management

As a senior manager, you will have many more meetings to chair than a middle manager. Many will be one-to-one encounters in which you will need to change your mind-set from one group of issues and personalities to another. For example, on Fridays I conduct many of my meetings and move from the world of software glitches in the assessment/reporting system through to worries that the librarian has about the theft of the *Guinness Book of Records*. After break-time it's exam entries for GCSE and our policy on invigilation, then on to staffing problems in the Inclusion Unit, ending the morning with the photocopying maintenance contract with the media resources manager. In each contrasting scenario, I have to use the skills we described in Chapter 4, monitor the other manager's narrative of events, in particular the way that they are relating to members of their team, whom I never meet with directly. I decide whether to offer advice, support or give firmer direction.

To make one-to-one meetings like this successful, one needs to create a sense of purpose. This is easy when people know exactly what they want to do with the team of teachers they are working with. My job is to question them about these intended actions and double-check the vital small detail. Very often a little probing from me prompts them to add or change the way they were planning something. For example, the assessment manager wanted to bring out Year 11 reports by a certain date. I reminded her to look at the school diary so she could pick a day on which most of the staff were not snowed under with Year 9 marking.

Very often the questions such as 'What about?' or 'Have you thought of?' are an excellent strategy to get the middle managers to be more lenient and humane on the staff they are managing. On other occasions my suggestions are designed to toughen up the head of department's organisation and set the staff more demanding work schedules. As we saw in Chapter 4, each manager brings their own individual set of strengths and weaknesses to the line-management meeting. They also have to lead and manage a completely 'one off' combination of staff personalities in their team.

Each of my weekly line-management meetings last up to thirty minutes and creates a running narrative of issues. Between line-management meetings, there are lots of quick informal interchanges about little steps forward and back. But the real exchange of ideas takes place in the meeting, which must be kept free of all interruptions. To achieve this, I try and follow three golden rules:

1. Book yourself line-management time so that neither party can be asked to do cover.
2. Shut your office door and don't answer the phone.
3. If people keep on trying to bother you, change the location of the meeting to a place where people won't expect to find you.

After line-management meetings, I write up a quick set of notes about the issues discussed and what each party has agreed to do about them before the next meeting in a week's time. There is no need to be more elaborate than that but the notes should be distributed quickly so they are available as an immediate aide-memoire for both parties.

Larger meetings

Larger meeting of staff are more clumsy and unwieldy than the regular one-to-one meetings where you get to know the idiosyncrasies of the person you work with and vice versa. To run them effectively, you need to think about the organisation much more carefully.

In large meetings, the increased number or personalities make them much more unpredictable and ground rules need to be established more firmly, each and every time. Here are some you should consider:

- Know what you are trying to achieve and be clear about the purpose of the meeting. Set the parameters with everybody at the beginning.
- Some meetings are for discussion, others for giving information or collecting it. Almost all meetings in school are consultative and few lead to an executive decision taken by the teaching staff voting. Headteachers usually have meetings to gauge the variety of opinions in the school, before deciding on their own, or with their senior team's advice, on what to do next.
- If you have a complex issue to analyse, make the meeting a one-item agenda.
- Hand out a proposal paper before the meeting so people have had a chance to consider the issues and a number of ways forward on them.
- Allow yourself to be personal as well as objective. Staff often want to focus on the way that a change will affect them as individuals.
- Think about the tone of your introduction and your responses. Being thoughtful and conciliatory will work better than sounding aggressive and cutting off other people's viewpoint.
- Meetings need to conclude with a summing-up statement. The people at the meeting cannot expect an instant decision on a complex issue, but should be told what the next step in the decision-making process will be.

Acting as headteacher for a day or longer

At some point, you will be probably have to be the acting headteacher. Sole primary school deputies will have this as a regular experience but at secondary school it will be less regular unless you are the senior deputy headteacher. Personally, I used to do it a lot in a small secondary school where I was the only deputy headteacher and I do it very occasionally in my current institution, a large comprehensive school with a big senior team, where I am the third deputy in the pecking order.

If you are doing it for a day you are essentially a 'site manager', trying to ensure that the school day goes smoothly. You will pass the baton back to the headteacher, without having to make more than a few organisational and disciplinary decisions to keep the show on the road. If anything very difficult blows up, you would usually be able to phone your headteacher or seek advice from other colleagues in middle or senior management.

If a day turns into days or a couple of weeks, you will have to increase the range of decisions you take and the advanced planning that you get involved in. When I was site manager at my present school for a day, I was conscious of the headteacher's clerical staff continuing to book appointments for his diary that involved his pre-determined agenda as the leader. I felt like a cuckoo in somebody else's nest as I sat in his massive office and took routine decisions that kept the school ticking over that day.

However, if you are acting headteacher for a period of a half term or longer, you will have to start leading in a much more comprehensive way. At the very least you will have to manage the implementation of regular calendar issues and planned innovations already on the school's Development Plan, increasingly using your own style of leadership rather than the absent headteacher's. Most plans need constant modification and/or evaluation and the longer you are in charge, the more they will become your own educational vision for the school's future. Increasingly, the administration and senior management teams will collaborate with your educational agenda. At this point you should demand a temporary enhancement of your salary to a headteacher's level.

Being an acting headteacher for even a short period of time is an interesting experience. In many ways, it is empowering. For the first time in your school career, it's you who decides which of a range of options to take. As a deputy, you have to take most significant issues to the headteacher, who decides what you should do. In a big secondary school, you often have to take problems to your fellow senior managers, who may or may not handle them to your liking. But as the site manager, you can decide on your own course of action and then channel the staffing into enacting it. Your priorities can become the school priorities. Obviously, this is a potentially exciting development for any deputy headteacher, although it also gives you responsibility for difficult decisions and for everything that goes wrong as well as right in your school. Not all deputy headteachers are happy with this remit as we shall see in Chapter 12. For those who are thinking of going on to headship, the chance to be a temporary headteacher is very useful.

Chapter 11

Learning to look after yourself

In this chapter we look at:

- the multi-tasking element of a school senior manager's job in terms of the pressure to function as a office administrator whilst simultaneously dealing with crowd-control situations;
- ways you can prioritise your work and organise your time to deal with the multi-task environment;
- the secretive and 'covert' strategies you might use to 'trick' the system and its heavy expectations on you so you can stay sane and still do a good job.

Surviving the multi-tasking environment

The incredible variety of work I am supposed to be handling simultaneously never fails to amaze me. A typical example occurred the other day. I was checking the rules that allow some newly arrived ethnic minority pupils exemption from the SATs league tables. As I walked across the playground, deep in thought about where the school would stand in terms of its value-added criteria this year as a result of this possible alteration, I walked straight into a hysterical mob of youngsters gathering around the stiff little body of a dead mouse. Some of the boys were trying to kick it at one of the girls, who were standing around screaming hysterically. One particularly odious Year 10 boy stooped down to pick up the dead mouse and fling it into the group of girls. SATs data forgotten, I jumped in and put my foot on the dead mouse. A couple of lads tried to push my foot off it, but I stood resolute. The crowd around me got bigger, feeding off the news that I had something horrible under my shoe. Somebody tried to push me from behind and I over-balanced, dropping all my work. A dreadful scream went up from the mob. 'It's a mouse, a mouse. He's squashing it.' Luckily, a fellow teacher came to my support and helped me pick up some of the sheets of my value-added data, whilst I struggled to conceal the mouse from the ever-growing crowd. I now wriggled my emergency mobile phone out of my inside pocket, keeping my foot over the animal and called up the premises team to come and relieve us of the body. I kept my foot over the mouse as my loyal colleague watched my back so nobody could try and push me again. In five minutes, the now very squashed mouse was brushed into a pan. Crisis over, and one particularly vital page of student data had blown away!

The juxtaposition of detailed intellectual work with energy-sapping crowd control is a key feature of senior management. Sometimes I know that its dangerous to step out of my office because I'll lose my high level of concentration on the curriculum report I'm writing in the deluge of disciplinary issues occurring in the corridor. Lesson changeovers and the end of lunchtime are especially volatile.

Given these extreme contradictions, some would say exciting variety in the job, senior managers need to protect themselves from being completely overrun and psychologically battered. If you don't take care of your own mental and physical well-being, nobody else will. Inner-city schools offer the most extreme divergences of experience – opportunities for calm, reflective administration and management are frequently lost to the uproarious physical and verbal maelstrom of the corridors and classroom. But there is always an element of this kind of work in any senior manager's role, whatever the type of school. The conflict between being proactive and reactive, trail-blazing new ideas and acting as a shock absorber remain a prevailing tension in your working life.

Here are other typical examples of these conflicting agendas, in which I literally found myself trying to do two jobs at the same time.

I attempt to tally the English GCSE results at E to G for the girls in last year's Year 11, whilst simultaneously dressing down a pupil who has been sent out to me from a science lesson. I moralise about his appalling behaviour, then ask him a question about how he intends to change it. As he sits, sullen and slightly tight-lipped, I do a quick tally of the grades, counting under my breath, thus completing what I had set out to do in the first place. 'I'm still waiting to hear what you've got to say for yourself,' I say, pretending to sound menacing, as I write in the final figure and inwardly sigh with relief at the statistical job completed.

Later that week I am not so lucky when checking to see whether we've got the right tiers of the maths SATs papers. As I rip open a delivery note, I am called to deal with a Year 10 pupil, lurching around the playground and suspected as 'drunk'. I bring him into my office. He doesn't deny that he has been drinking as he collapses over the box of National Curriculum level 4–7 exam papers. But when I say I am going to send him home to sober up, he gets highly agitated at the idea that his father will be told the truth about his sudden 'illness'. He pleads with me not to tell his father what has happened. Returning to my count of maths papers is now impossible as I try and coax him into accepting my authority and he tries to lurch out of the office and back into the playground. In the end I calm him sufficiently to get him to slump in a seat next to a plastic bowl, perched on the Teachers Instructions on SATs. Luckily the bowl is not needed, as he shows no signs of throwing up, and I am able to go off to discuss the wording of the letter that will be sent home with him with the headteacher. She agrees that we need to get him off-site and that we can be evasive about the exact cause of his illness, just to get him home. One hour later, I am completely exhausted from the fraught negotiations to get him off the premises and the intricate exam checking has been postponed, yet again.

Given the extreme pressures that can be put on a senior manager, it's important to look at all the ways you can protect yourself against such high levels of stress.

Time management

To survive and succeed with a large job description, you have to ask the one central question, many times a day: Does it have to be done now (as in right now, or could it be done later today)? The kinds of problems to which the answer to the question is 'yes' can be classified as 'urgent'. A fight definitely falls into the 'urgent' category, as does a bullying incident, in which you promise to report back the results of your initial investigations to angry parents.

But just because something is 'urgent' doesn't necessarily make it 'important'. The really 'important' tasks are all too easily postponed for an avalanche of 'urgent' problems. The 'important' are often jobs around slow-burn curriculum development, evaluation of the school policy on bullying or discussion of the SMT rota for patrolling corridors during lessons. 'Important' work often requires proactivity and initiative, leading it to be regularly displaced by the 'urgent' – reactive 'fire-fighting' work.

Yet to be a truly effective senior manager, you need to maintain a balance between the short-term 'urgent' and the longer-term 'important'. Indeed, if you can make significant parts of the 'important' function well, there will be less of the 'urgent' to deal with anyway.

Making your own deadlines

Given that schools always have something to react to, it's best to plan well ahead, whenever you can, so you leave that spare capacity for unexpected problems. For example, if I've planned my assembly well ahead of time and written up my action plan on mentoring in advance, it isn't a complete disaster when I'm called unexpectedly to calm the lunch queue or an angry parent.

Pushing aside trivia

Each and every day, trivia needs to be actively pushed aside – back to the bottom of the in-tray or, better still, the bottom of the bin. Every day, try and find a little time to do some medium-term planning for what you really want to achieve over the next few weeks.

File it or throw it

Give yourself about fifteen minutes a day deciding whether to file something or throw it away. This stops you from making incredibly messy piles of paper everywhere, for all the issues you couldn't quite make up your mind over.

Despite all the information technology systems, schools are still full of paper. Spending time on setting up proper filing systems, and using them regularly, is vital. Filing may not be a glamorous occupation but the next time you need to find something, knowing where it is can save a lot of time and anxiety.

Prioritising your work

In order to avoid the multi-tasking nightmares I described at the beginning of the chapter, you must learn to prioritise your work carefully. Some jobs need proper quiet time to think them through. Although thinking and document drafting could take place at home, there will be occasions when you should try and override the typical senior manager's day of constant interruptions and short bursts of concentration, to do proper writing in school.

Another excellent way to prioritise is to break down a complex task into a lot of smaller, more manageable steps, so you take the stress out of the work you are doing.

Try not to procrastinate

We all try to postpone things we don't like doing, the things we find difficult or boring. But as deputy headteacher you are supposed to be sufficiently self-aware to compensate for your own shortcomings. I try and trick myself into dealing with the things I don't like doing, in the following ways:

1 Schedule the difficult, important and unpleasant tasks first.
2 Set a deadline publically so you've committed yourself to the staff.
3 Don't worry about doing it absolutely perfectly but instead set a level of sufficient completion for a task so you can move on with a clear conscience.

Emergency action to protect yourself

Prioritising in the way I have suggested will usually be enough to bring back a sense of order and job satisfaction to the school day. But in very challenging schools, more drastic steps are needed to protect yourself from meltdown. The suggestions we have looked at so far are a 'gentleman's' guide to staying sane, but sometimes desperate circumstances call for more desperate measures. Here is a guide to ten strategies to conduct clandestine warfare against the system – a system that will suck your blood mercilessly if you play it straight as a senior manager, each and every day.

The 'covert' action plan

1. Keep an eye on yourself throughout the day. Try and map a route through the day that prioritises some things in the in-tray, but leaves plenty of time and energy for the unexpected. Be prepared to made big changes as the day progresses: as a deputy headteacher, you can't avoid some of the unexpected. But look after yourself and your mental and physical well-being. 'You', not the job description, are the number one priority. If necessary, drop virtually everything in the in-tray if you need recovery time from a very difficult situation such as an abusive parent or a violent crowd-control situation.
2. Never get back to educational bureaucrats the first time they ring you, unless they are people whom you respect and are giving something genuinely useful to the school. Otherwise, the third phone message will do fine. Then, pretend to co-operate but do the minimum you can get away with. Book them in at long intervals and keep them at arm's length. You can't deal with all the bureaucratic initiatives. Lead on the main ones, and try and do those properly. Delegate others into oblivion.
3. Try and delegate anything that you don't think is vitally important. But bear in mind, some things that are 'dross' still have to be done by you – for appearances. You will have to drop some of your good ideas and waste precious time with some half-baked initiatives that you need to be seen to be doing, but which are really central government or LEA displacement activity.
4. Give yourself time and space in the school day to sit down, have a chat and 'chill out' a bit.
5. If you are getting steamed up, try to postpone absolutely non-essential work immediately and prioritise 'looking after yourself'. You need a ' time out' at this point to get the job back into real perspective: the perspective that brings us back down to earth and reminds us that nothing is so important that it can't wait. Concentrate on looking for that all-important relaxation time and avoid snapping back at pupils, parents and colleagues.
6. Be sneaky about finding ways to look after yourself. When you are feeling stressed, don't pick up the phone, let people leave a voice message, then you can decide to get back to them later or not at all. This is better than a knee-jerk reaction that is more likely to be irritable or angry.

7 Leave school early for a run, a swim or some other form of physical exercise, if you feel big pressure building up. This is not skiving, it is vital recovery time and will pay dividends in the long run. How often are the most efficient workers the ones who spend the longest time stewing away on the school site at the end of the day?
8 Duck and dive a bit. Don't feel that every kid who is hanging around or every unruly incident is one that you must personally intervene in. Turn a blind eye and metaphorically 'hide in your office' sometimes. Don't rush to be the first on gate duty at the end of school when you have already had a belly-full of unpleasant confrontations that day.
9 Sometimes you will have to accept that proactive work that might actually be useful must be dropped for pointless and futile meetings with various agencies, advisers, initiative-makers etc., just so you can be seen to be doing your job. Being seen to be doing your job in the topsy-turvy world of education is always more important than actually doing it. So attend some of the silly meetings or ineffectual training sessions, especially if they are in school time, so you can have some respite from the stressful corridor patrols and crowd control.
10 When somebody is trying to bend your ear about something, a useful reply is to say that it sounds like a great idea and can they get something in writing for you. That will put off all but the most determined.

Socialising and making friends while in senior management

It's lonely at the top. I have found it increasingly so as one of the deputy headteachers in a large comprehensive school. The good friendships I had as a middle manager in my last school have not been possible in the last two years in senior management of a new one.

Three things stand out that make senior management very different:

Firstly, you have more non-contact time than other staff, who largely do 'back to back' teaching. This means your day has a different routine and daily cycle. For example, at lunchtime and immediately after school I go into action, dealing with large numbers of pupils, sometimes in stressful situations. But these are often times when my teaching-bound colleagues are grabbing a well-earned communal rest and having a chat.

Secondly, there is the intimacy factor that comes with close team working. Middle managers and ordinary teachers work alongside their colleagues in departments. These teaching teams share the same type of highs and lows in the classroom. They can 'bitch' about how useless and distant senior management is and have some honest discourse on the shortcomings of school policy. For the senior management it is rather different. Its members are expected to hold their tongue on decisions, for the sake of cabinet loyalty, even when they think they are misguided. It is probably human nature that senior team members occasionally compete for the patronage and good favour of the headteacher. This can inhibit the development of real friendship.

But thirdly and finally, the most serious problem of all: just in case you thought I could cast my friendship net wider than my immediate small group of senior colleagues, think again. When you find a way of getting out of SMT patrol and sit down at break-time with the rest of the staff, people just don't talk to you like they used to. The price of being in the controlling hierarchy is to expect conversations to stop when you come into earshot. When sitting down, it is all too easy to be drawn into a 'work only' conversation. You can find yourself being lobbied about this or that school issue, or worse still, rather than relaxing, you find you are initiating a networking session with teachers you wanted to talk to about something managerial. It's no surprise to find that such conversations don't break through the work roles and can't get personal enough to help you relax with staff and make friends.

Strategies to reduce senior management isolation

1. Make time to sit with colleagues so you give yourself the opportunity to start making friends.
2. Go into the staff room at break-time and lunchtime for at least a few minutes, even if you are supposed to be on duty. Sit down at the end of the school day and chat to people when they are winding down.
3. Don't talk shop all the time or you'll never get to know anybody properly.

Chapter 12

What's next?

In this chapter we look at:

- the NPQH as a useful way of finding out if you are interested in becoming a headteacher;
- undertaking further school training on finance and budget;
- the advantages and disadvantages of staying as a deputy headteacher;
- other possible career paths for those who don't want to step up to headship.

Is headship the right step for you?

In almost all the job descriptions you will see for senior management, one of the essential person specification criteria is to have the ambition to go on to headship. Is it really a prerequisite for an assistant or deputy headteacher to aspire to be headteacher of a school? Many of you would not have joined a senior management team if you did not have this in the back of your mind. The first step for the assistant headteachers among you will be to become deputy headteachers with a wider strategic remit before thinking of applying for headship.

It is logical that you would want to develop along this learning curve. After all, as a senior manager you will have gained experience of running whole-school curriculum development and line managing large teams of people. Most primary and some secondary deputies will have had regular daily experience of running the school when the headteacher is off-site. In some cases, they will have acted as headteacher for periods of time. So surely the next natural step is to take on the running of all aspects of school life and gain the freedom to lead and manage in ways you feel comfortable with. Up to now, you will have been following the overall vision of your boss – the headteacher. You may well have had to compromise a lot of what you believe in when following their educational vision and leadership style. But despite those potentially frustrating limitations, you have also been spared the chilly winds of being on the summit on one's own, accountable for every little thing that goes on in the school. As a senior manager you don't have to take difficult decisions, anything tricky can be referred to your headteacher for their final say so. A deputy had a wonderful get-out clause which always makes life a lot easier. It's the explanation they always have available to them in difficult situations: 'The head decided that we've got to do it like this.' If the staff trust you to have represented their points of view strongly to the headteacher over controversial decisions, this statement absolves you from any further responsibility for them. As a senior manager who steps up to be headteacher, you lose this safety net.

To counterbalance the disadvantages of full accountability and difficult decision-making, promotion to headship gives more power to determine the direction of the school. Headteachers have the freedom to delegate much of the practical daily organisation to their senior team and free themselves up to concentrate on what they think is important.

Clearly, the additional freedoms and significantly higher salary of a headteacher have failed to convince many experienced deputies to step up into headship. At the time of writing this book, both the primary and secondary sectors were having problems filling headships.

Senior managers who want to be headteachers

NPQH

The National Professional Qualification in Headship (NPQH) will soon be compulsory for all aspiring headteachers. It is useful training for those who are eager to become headteachers but it is also helpful experience for those who aren't sure. The course focuses the participants on the key issues of school strategic management and gives them a chance to study theories of leadership. It encourages senior managers to be proactive in setting up major whole-school curriculum initiatives and follow them through. But most usefully, prospective headteachers are introduced to one of the most jealously guarded secrets of their bosses, the financial management of the school budget. Very few deputies gained access to this vital aspect of a headteacher's job description before the NPQH was introduced. Now they can get some experience of how a budget is constructed.

Further experience of financial management

Further training on financial management beyond the NPQH would also be useful for aspiring headteachers. As deputies it would be very useful to sit in on the governor's finance committee and see how your headteacher links the overall budget to key features in the school development plan and how monthly spending is monitored.

Senior managers who don't want to be headteachers

There is no reason why you shouldn't stay a member of a senior management team rather than become its overall leader. However, the longer you stay in a particular position in one school, the harder it becomes to make a parallel move from one deputy headship to another. This is due to the prevailing expectation that every deputy should want to be a headteacher and if they don't, their personality and drive must be somehow lacking.

If you become a 'career' deputy or assistant headteacher, you can have a positive and interesting time modifying aspects of your job description over the years. Change becomes inevitable if you find yourself working for a new headteacher with a different educational vision and personality. But staying in one school as a senior manager over a period of time can produce a negative cycle of events. You could get stale or find a new headteacher pushing you to assume roles that make you anxious and uncomfortable.

Avenues other than headship

Experience of school senior management is a major advantage in moving into management posts in local education authorities or the increasing number of private educational companies. Key roles include general inspector (school improvement adviser) and borough-wide management of government initiatives on, for example, literacy, numeracy and behaviour. The salaries are the same or slightly higher than deputy headteacher's leadership points. From there, the career structure can take you up to senior local education management with salaries similar to some headteachers.

Careers in the education bureaucracy have far less daily accountability than headteacher. If a school gets bad results, the headteacher not the link educational adviser takes the blame. But by equal measure, inspectors and advisers often have a very marginal role in changing the practice of the schools they work in. As we have already seen, many headteachers, senior managers and ordinary teachers treat them with a mixture of caution and disdain. Being regarded as a necessary evil that must be put up with limits the appeal of an advisory post to many dynamic school practitioners.

Increasingly, senior managers with particular specialities for behaviour management or a particular style of teaching are setting themselves up as independent consultants and going into school under private contract. A closer look at their background shows that they have often worked in advisory posts in local authorities after leaving schools. They often work part time, supplementing their consultancy role with a pension from previous full-time public employment.

Conclusion

Most effective assistant and deputy headteachers command a strong hand in most of the following personal qualities and skills. How many of them sum up your character?

Personal skills needed to interact effectively with your staff

Being good at:

- listening
- negotiating
- chairing meetings
- enthusing
- being creative
- servicing and supporting others
- analysing problems
- speaking to large audiences of teachers or pupils.

Personal qualities that accompany these skills

- tact
- empathy
- sensitivity
- patience
- enthusiasm
- flexibility
- versatility
- sense of humour

- optimism
- tenacity in the pursuit of a goal
- stamina in the face of long working hours and stress
- being decisive, when necessary
- sticking to difficult decisions.

It is impossible for anybody to demonstrate all of these personal qualities and skills in equal measure, all of the time. But it's vital to have the majority most of the time, along with a keen appreciation of your weaknesses and how you can stop them spoiling your overall performance.

For example, I am sufficiently aware of my weaknesses to partially blunt their ill effects, even though I can't always conquer them completely. When I get tired and stressed by long hours or a multiplicity of tasks coming at me at the same time, I can show my frustration by being impatient with colleagues and 'snapping' at them. I now recognise the warning signals and try to follow the advice I have given you in this book about taking 'covert action' to reduce stress levels quickly. But on the occasions when it doesn't work, there is no choice but to admit to one's mistake after the event and apologise quickly.

My second major weakness is that I am very impatient with outside agencies, local authority advisers and central government directives that threaten to take time away from the goals that I have prioritised. I am most likely to 'snap' at these outsiders, when I believe that are peddling superficial solutions to complex educational problems. I try and limit my exposure to them and adapt only the best of their external plans to fit in with my internal priorities.

My third and greatest weakness comes about from one of my real strengths, being naturally open-minded and a good listener: I can find it hard come to a decision, seeing the pros and cons of both sides of an argument. I try and get round the problem by taking important decisions after I have heard detailed evidence from all sides. But the hardest decisions for me are the ones that have to be taken very quickly. I am beginning to learn that for those kind of decisions, you just have to take a deep breath and go with your gut feeling. As a deputy headteacher, I can usually rely on working an issue through with the headteacher. As a headteacher, I would need to find a new way of seeking advice and guidance from trusted members of the senior management team.

Luckily, I am not afflicted by the biggest of all deficiencies a senior manager can have, being so self-important and full of themselves that they can't see or won't admit to any weakness.

Let's conclude by summing up the essential qualities a senior manager needs to survive and succeed in the twenty-first-century school. We need people who can stay relaxed with the people they manage and don't let the constant initiative culture of the school improvement agenda distort their own belief system. Maintaining faith in one's own educational ideas is vital, as those of us who have been in school leadership for long enough will have observed that 'what goes round, comes round!' Just one current example from among many demonstrates this principle. Fifteen years ago, the National Curriculum was introduced and everybody had to follow a prescribed diet. Now we are moving away from a fixed curriculum for 14–16-year-olds and loosening subject specificity for the 11-year-olds. I remember when integrated studies for Year 7 was the fashion with its blend of English, geography, history and religious studies. It was brought in as a strategy for emulating primary school conditions for longer by giving one class the same teacher for up to ten hours a week. But when the National Curriculum arrived in the early 1990s with its insistence that each school subject be taught by a specialist, the Year 7 lessons were split up again. Now, in the early twenty-first century, many schools are being encouraged to introduce an integrated curriculum taught by one teacher again for the first year of secondary schooling.

So educational changes swing from one side to the other, like a see-saw going up and down. The good senior manager will keep their balance by making sure that positive relationships with the staff and pupils remain their central priority at all times. Schools are too busy and stressful for you to be anything but humane to the people you lead and manage. Being humane often means finding compromises in difficult situations and maintaining the staff's goodwill, so that you maximise their talents and minimise their weaknesses.

Index